Guantánamo

Guantánamo

The War on Human Rights

David Rose

THE NEW PRESS

NEW YORK
LONDON

Requests for permission to reproduce selections from this book should be mailed to:
Permissions Department, The New Press, 38 Greene Street, New York, NY 10013

Published in the United States by The New Press, New York, 2004
Distributed by W. W. Norton & Company, Inc., New York

ISBN 1-56584-957-4 (hc.)
CIP data available

The New Press was established in 1990 as a not-for-profit alternative to the large,
commercial publishing houses currently dominating the book publishing industry.
The New Press operates in the public interest rather than for private gain, and is
committed to publishing, in innovative ways, works of educational, cultural, and
community value that are often deemed insufficiently profitable.

www.thenewpress.com

Printed in the United States of America

10   9   8   7   6   5   4   3   2   1

To Carolyn
forever

CONTENTS

ACKNOWLEDGMENTS

The genesis of this book was an article I wrote for the January 2004 issue of *Vanity Fair,* and my first debt is to the magazine's editor, Graydon Carter, who had the idea of sending me to Cuba in the first place. I must also thank Michael Hogan, my young and brilliant editor in New York, and Henry Porter, the magazine's London editor, for their guidance and support. I first interviewed the returned British detainees for the London *Observer,* and special thanks are due to its editor, Roger Alton, and deputy editor, Paul Webster, who have been colleagues and comrades for more than twenty years.

Blame for the genesis of the expansion and transformation of these articles lies with Colin Robinson, editorial director of The New Press. My warmest thanks to him, and to Neil Belton, who after taking on a U.K. edition for Faber & Faber, made editorial suggestions of great value. I must also thank my agents in London (Peter Robinson) and New York (Jill Grinberg), who have been patient and loyal for many years.

I want to record my deep appreciation for the long-standing friendship of Clive Stafford Smith, whose hand, directly or indirectly, has helped to guide my own throughout much of the text that follows. As a Soros senior fellow, he has played a central role in creating a global network committed to fighting for justice at Guantánamo. With his usual generosity, he passed on this network of contacts—and much else besides—to me.

Many others also helped, as sources, tutors and as readers of parts of the manuscript. Some I cannot name, but in no particular order, I would like publicly to thank A. Sivanandan, Don Rehkopf, Jamie Fellner, Steven Watt, Carol Rosenberg, Tammy Audi, Daryl Matthews, Tony Christino, Louise Christian, Kaveh Moussavi, Bernhard Docke, Dalia Hashad, Vaughan Lowe, Emily Whitefield, Gareth Peirce, Hussein Zahir, Michael Ratner, Tim Winter, Tom Williamson, Milton Bearden, Gisli Gudjonsson, Chris Anderson, and especially the returned British detainees, Shafiq Rasul, Asif Iqbal, Ruhal Ahmed and Tarek Dergoul.

I must thank the public affairs staff of the Joint Task Force at Guantánamo Bay, especially Lieutenant Colonel Pam Hart and her successor, Lieutenant Colonel Leon Sumpter, who always tried to be as helpful as their orders would permit. I would also like to pay special tribute to a few good men and one woman: the military judge advocates assigned by the Pentagon as defense lawyers for Guantánamo detainees, who have fought their clients' corners with fearless determination: Lieutenant Commander Charlie Swift, Major Michael Mori, Colonel Sharon Shaffer, Philip Sundel and Major Mark Bridges.

Finally, I express my heartfelt thanks and love for my wife, Carolyn, who gave birth to a real baby, our second son Daniel, when this one was just starting to gestate.

David Rose
Oxford, July 2004

Guantánamo

INTRODUCTION

JUSTICE JACKSON: Protective custody meant that you were taking people into custody who had not committed any crimes but who, you thought, might possibly commit a crime?

HERMANN GOERING: Yes. People were arrested and taken into protective custody who had not yet committed any crime, but who could be expected to do so if they remained free . . . the original reason for creating the concentration camps was to keep there such people whom we rightfully considered enemies of the state.

—The Trial of Hermann Goering, Nuremburg, 1946

The military aircraft in which Asif Iqbal and Shafiq Rasul sat chained to a bench, soaked in their own urine, earmuffed, masked and unable to see, landed at the American airstrip at Guantánamo Bay, Cuba, on January 14, 2002. The two men, who had traveled to Pakistan from their homes in Britain five months earlier in order to attend Iqbal's wedding, had already survived a massacre by their original captors, the private army of the Afghan warlord Rashid Dostum, and they were filthy and half-starved. As their seemingly interminable flight ground on, they remained unaware of their destination. But to the rest of the world, its name had recently become very familiar.

The first contingent of alleged Taliban and al-Qaeda prisoners had reached the new detention camp at Guantánamo—GTMO, or "Gitmo," as the U.S. military usually terms it—from Kandahar in Afghanistan three days earlier. During the preceding week, marines had labored to build their makeshift prison, Camp X-ray: a dozen rows of steel mesh cages, open to the elements, ringed by a razor-wire fence. On arrival, the detainees had been led into its compound and photographed as they waited to be processed. Shackled hand and foot, dressed in orange jumpsuits, still wearing the black-lensed goggles, surgical masks, headphones and taped-on gloves that they had been forced to don at the start of their twenty-seven-hour flight, the detainees knelt in the Gitmo dust as crew-cut servicemen loomed in threatening poses over them. Within a few days, U.S. Defense Secretary Donald Rumsfeld would regret allowing these pictures to be released: to have done so, he said, was "probably unfortunate." The front-page headline used with the photos in Britain's conservative *Daily Mail* typified responses outside the United States. It consisted of a single word: TORTURE!

The photographs conveyed a sense of fear and dehumanization, messages underlined by the comments of those who commanded Gitmo's jailers. The prisoners, said General Richard E. Myers, chairman of the Joint Chiefs of Staff, had had to be restrained in this fashion because they were so dangerous and bent on destruction that given half a chance, they "would gnaw through hydraulic lines in the back of a C-17 to bring it down." The inference was unmistakable: Osama bin Laden, al-Qaeda's elusive leader, might still be at large, but here were some of his key lieutenants, men who shared direct responsibility for the attacks on New York and Washington of September 11, 2001. Although they had been captured in Afghanistan, a place where America was at war, Rumsfeld said they would not be viewed in legal terms as prisoners of war, but as "unlawful combatants." As such, he went on, "they do not have any rights under the Geneva Conventions." Nor, as foreign nationals held outside the United States, would they have any recourse to American courts. The Pentagon's power over them appeared to be absolute. In due course, some of the prisoners would face trial by a military commission and, eventually, the death penalty.

As individuals, the prisoners had ceased to exist. A reporter asked Rumsfeld if they included any known terrorist kingpins. The defense secretary replied that he had no idea: "I don't even know their names."

The few journalists who witnessed the first detainees' arrival in Cuba, and later the second contingent including Iqbal and Rasul, were kept at a distance. "One by one, manacled and masked, the first 20 of up to perhaps 2,000 Taliban and al-Qaeda prisoners arrived in this sweltering U.S. military outpost on Friday—four months to the day after the Sept. 11 attacks," wrote *The Miami Herald*'s Carol Rosenberg, Guantánamo's most assiduous chronicler during the camp's first year. "The military left nothing to chance. They ringed the aircraft on the leeward side of this sprawling base with Marines in Humvees, some armed with rocket launchers, others with heavy machine guns. A Navy Huey helicopter hovered overhead, a gunner hanging off the side."

These precautions were essential, Marine Brigadier General Michael Lehnert told reporters shortly before the detainees' plane touched down: "These represent the worst elements of al-Qaeda and the Taliban. We asked for the bad guys first." Some reports claimed, somewhat improbably, that detainees had struggled with their guards as they disembarked from the plane. Rosenberg quoted Major Steve Cox refuting them: "No, quite to the contrary. They were wobbly and disoriented." Cox said the prisoners' goggles were blacked out "for security reasons," and their masks were to protect their guards against possible tuberculosis.

She went on to describe the detainees' new home at Camp X-ray. "Each man is confined to one cell, a mat on a concrete block floor, and gets a bucket in which to relieve himself. The camp warden said MPs [military police] would lead them, one by one, to latrines as need be, and conceded that when it rains, some will get wet. Other supplies they will receive, described by Cox as 'comfort items,' include two bath towels, one to use for bathing, the other to serve as a prayer mat; toothpaste and brush; soap and shampoo, plus flip-flops for footwear. 'They get the two towels but no blanket,' the major said."

General Lehnert told Rosenberg that the detainees would be free to practice their religion and would be given *halal,* food without pork. She was shown an example: "A vacuum-packed vegetable-and-pasta dish, plus an accessory pack that included peanuts, a granola bar and a box of Froot Loops."

Reporters have never been allowed to speak with the prisoners at Guantánamo, and the few that have tried have been summarily expelled. It was, therefore, not until many months later, when some had been released, that one could obtain a description of the journey to Guantánamo from the point of view of detainees. Iqbal and Rasul, both in their early twenties, were born and raised in Tipton, a small industrial town in Britain's west Midlands. Having spent more than two years in Cuba, in which time they underwent some 200 interrogation sessions, they were finally deemed not to represent the worst elements of al-Qaeda after all and were repatriated in March 2004.

Before their flight to Cuba, they told me, they had been woken early in their tent at Kandahar. Their clothes were cut off and their beards and hair shaved with electric clippers. Then, naked, they were made to squat, while a soldier performed an anal search. "He used no lubricant," Iqbal said. "It was painful and humiliating." Afterward, they were dressed in their jumpsuits and their hands were first cuffed, then gloved, with duct tape used to stick the gloves to their wrists. According to Rasul, "It was roasting hot. They made us sit outside in the sun on some gravel while they processed everyone—for like ten hours."

Throughout this time, they said, they were given no water. A few minutes before they were loaded into the aircraft, they were given one of the military's "M.R.E.s," a meal ready to eat, but consuming this airline-style tray without utensils while gloved and shackled was not easy. "I tried to bend over and eat it like an animal," Iqbal said. Their handcuffs were attached to a waistbelt and leg irons, an arrangement that was to become very familiar, which they came to describe as a "three-piece suit." Rasul said he complained that his chains were too tight, but a guard replied: "You'll live."

Just before embarkation, the masks, muffs and goggles were applied. En route, they were each given a sandwich, but there was no opportunity to have their bonds removed in order to visit the toilet. Iqbal said: "Basically, people wet their pants." The only break was a two-hour stopover at an American base in Turkey. Blind and deaf, Rasul said, "The only thing that occupied me was that I was in serious pain. The guards told me to go to sleep, but the belt was digging into my side. When I finally got to Cuba, I found I was bleeding. I lost feeling in my hands for the next six months."

When the aircraft doors opened, they still had not been told where they were going. "All I knew was that I was somewhere with intense heat," Rasul said. "An American voice shouted: 'I am Sergeant so-and-so, U.S. Marine Corps, you are arriving at your final destination.'" The Gitmo airstrip lies a three-mile ferry journey across the bay from the detention camp, a journey the prisoners made in a school bus. Iqbal said: "The boat was moving in the swell, making the bus rock, and the American guy says: 'Stop moving.' I couldn't stop, so he hit me." Rasul made the mistake of telling a guard he was English. "Traitor!" the guard yelled.

At last they arrived at Camp X-ray. "The sun was beating down and the sweat was pouring into my eyes," said Rasul. "I shouted for a doctor, someone poured water into my eyes and then I heard it again: 'Traitor, traitor.'" It took more than four hours for the marines to go through the paperwork, deal with each detainee and allot him a cage, and throughout this time, those still waiting were forced to remain kneeling. Iqbal said: "I couldn't take the pain—this guy came to give me water, and basically, I had a fit. I fell over onto the floor so they took me into the processing place and gave me an intravenous glucose drip."

He recalled the moment his goggles were finally removed. "I look up and I see all these other people who hadn't yet been processed in orange suits and goggles and I think: 'I'm hallucinating.'"

Rasul was the last one processed, and by the time he got to his cage it was dark. First he was stripped naked and, still wearing his goggles and chains, was given a piece of soap and told to shower. When his goggles were finally removed, he peered through the tropical night at the cacti and razor wire and low scrubby hills beyond. Mosquitoes buzzed and bit. "I looked around and I thought, 'What the hell is this place?' "

This book attempts to answer this question and to examine some additional ones. Who are the prisoners at Guantánamo, and what is their detention *for*? What is its place in the so-called war on terror, and how effectively is it fulfilling its intended mission? How far has it measured up to the claims made about it and its inmates by leading figures in George W. Bush's administration?

It does not pretend to be comprehensive: For example, it considers the experience of prisoners from only a few of the forty-plus countries represented at Guantánamo. I have not had the chance to interview freed detainees from countries other than Britain. But the book is drawn from diverse sources, and I hope it identifies the most important issues raised by America's Gitmo experiment. In the autumn of 2003, I became one of more than 250 journalists to have visited Gitmo, initially for an article published in *Vanity Fair*. I tried to keep my eyes open and spoke to many soldiers and officials there, on and off the record, and I followed up my trip with interviews in Washington and elsewhere. I have made some limited use of the work of other journalists, and conducted extensive interviews with four of the five freed British detainees. I have also acquired some important internal documents from the Gitmo Joint Task Force, some of which are quoted in these pages for the first time. They are not classified: I am not disclosing secrets here that might damage America's cause in its war against terror. But they do shed further light on some of the camp's history and inner workings, information that some might prefer to keep hidden.

In the minds of many people, the first, extraordinary official statements about Gitmo will have proven to be durable. A writer who seeks to elicit concern about the human and legal rights of men such as Iqbal and Rasul, or sympathy for their suffering during twenty-six months at Gitmo, must first confront the assertions made by Donald Rumsfeld and others in the first months of 2002. "These people are committed terrorists," he said in response to the rising tide of international criticism of Guantánamo on January 21. "We are keeping them off the street and out of the airlines and out of nuclear power plants and out of ports across this country and across other countries." They were, he added during a visit to Gitmo at the start of the following month, "among the most dangerous, best-trained, vicious killers on the face of the earth." In Afghanistan, he said, "we were able to capture and detain a large number of people who had been through terrorist training camps and had learned a whole host of skills as to how they could kill innocent people, not how they could kill other soldiers. We've got a good slug of those folks off the street where they can't kill more people."

According to Vice President Dick Cheney: "These are the worst of a very bad lot. They are very dangerous. They are devoted to killing millions of Americans, innocent Americans, if they can, and they are perfectly prepared to die in the effort."

Rumsfeld accused those who had voiced anxieties on behalf of the detainees in the wake of the jumpsuit photographs—including the International Committee of the Red Cross, the European Union and Amnesty International—of indulging in "armchair hyperbole." Whatever impression the photographs may have conveyed, he said, "I am telling you what I believe in every inch of my body to be the truth . . . I haven't found a single scrap of any kind of information that suggests that anyone has been treated anything other than humanely." His critics should bear in mind that the detainees had "been involved in an effort to kill thousands of ordinary Americans."

This book will seek to refute these claims. Few of the approximately 750 individuals who have passed through Guantánamo or are still imprisoned there were devoted to killing Americans in any active sense, and the people who really fit this description now in U.S. custody have never been detained in Cuba. The evidence suggests that large numbers of the Gitmo prisoners—running into the hundreds—were absolutely innocent of the least involvement with anything that could reasonably be described as terrorist activity. They ended up in Cuba as a result of military intelligence screening procedures in Afghanistan and elsewhere that were flawed and inadequate, made still worse by the use of woefully poor and virtually untrained translators.

At a deeper level, they were there because of the way an American administration, which was already isolationist and disinclined to fetter its autonomy through treaties and international law, responded to the world's worst terrorist attacks. Before September 11, 2001, President Bush had repudiated the Kyoto treaty on global warming, indicated his desire to tear up agreements on ballistic missile defense, and declined to participate in the new International Criminal Court. In the wake of the enormous blow to the American psyche that the attacks represented, his decision that the war on terror would be fought according to new rules of his own administration's devising seems to have been almost a reflex. As White House Chief Counsel Alberto Gonzalez put it in a memo to Bush on January 25, 2002, "The war against terrorism is a new kind of war," in which there would be no place for old-fashioned strictures such as the Geneva Convention on the treatment of prisoners of war. According to Gonzalez, the war on terror rendered Geneva "obsolete." The English Court of Appeal once memorably described Guantánamo Bay as a "legal black hole," beyond the reach of any jurisdiction. As I show in chapter one, that was exactly its creators' point.

And Rumsfeld's claim that detainees have always been treated "humanely" can no longer be regarded as credible. Even if one ignored the mounting weight of personal testimony from those who have been released, there is the evidence of widespread mental deterioration reported by, among others, the Red Cross. To that—in the shadow of the scandal of prisoner abuse and torture at Abu Ghraib prison in Iraq that broke in the spring of 2004—must be added the Pentagon's admissions that physical and psychological coercion have formed part of the normal interrogation repertoire at Guantánamo Bay and that Rumsfeld personally authorized their use. According to the draft of a March 2003 memo to Rumsfeld by a working group led by the Pentagon's general counsel, William J. Haynes, normal prohibitions against torture need not apply at Guantánamo because nothing was more important than "obtaining intelligence vital to the protection of untold thousands of American citizens." The memo went on to advance a series of arguments to justify conduct that would normally merit criminal prosecution—what it called "legal doctrines . . . that could render specific conduct, otherwise criminal, not unlawful."

At the time of writing, after Abu Ghraib, there are signs that the complacency and insouciance, which initially marked many

American responses to any kind of criticism of the conduct of the war on terror, are beginning to evaporate. The victim-as-warrior mentality that swept the United States after 9/11 appears to be giving way to a climate in which it is becoming possible to address the morality of an institution such as Gitmo; to ask whether holding such numbers in such conditions outside the scope of the rule of law truly serves the values that the American nation and its Constitution seek to represent. On June 29, 2004, the U.S. Supreme Court took the first, vital steps toward limiting what had been the exercise of untrammeled executive power when it overruled the administration's position and decided that Gitmo prisoners did after all have rights under federal law, and they could use the courts to challenge their detention.

However, this book's most important argument is not legal or moral but pragmatic. Is Guantánamo, with its vast costs—in treasure, in effort and human resources, and to America's standing in the wider world—a justifiable means to the end of defeating Islamist terror? My answer, bleakly, is no. Gitmo's boosters, above all its former commandant, General Geoffrey Miller, at the time of writing the man in charge of Abu Ghraib, have claimed repeatedly that Gitmo has provided a rich harvest of "enormously valuable intelligence," which has prevented further terrorist attacks and laid al-Qaeda low. Serving and recently retired intelligence officers with direct access to Gitmo's "product" have told me that this is at best wishful thinking.

Meanwhile, if Guantánamo has provided but a few meager scraps of information, it has also become an icon of oppression throughout the developing—and especially the Muslim—world. Across the Middle East, those pictures of the newly arrived detainees kneeling in the dirt in their shackles have become a trope for cartoonists and pamphleteers, a graphic rendition of oppression that speaks to millions of Muslims. The unjust suffering of families and individuals engendered by this aspect of Operation Enduring Freedom is sowing dragons' teeth, turning moderates into fanatics determined to smite the West. Thirty years ago, the United Kingdom's use of detention without trial against the Provisional IRA in Ulster proved to be the best recruiting sergeant the terrorists ever knew, as the government's own assessments later admitted. Although the policy was ended after less than two years, it led directly to the bloodiest phase of Northern Ireland's troubles, and a period, in the mid-1970s, when the province was effectively beyond control.

The grievances created then took years to begin to dissipate, and they have not been forgotten. Guantánamo is having a similar, radicalizing effect in the Islamic world today. The case that Gitmo is legally and morally questionable has been well rehearsed. According to the terms of its own stated mission—to stop further terrorist attacks—it is ineffective, and its legacy may be written in blood.

1

HONOR BOUND

The United States is proud to call itself a nation ruled by law. But even a nation of laws must understand the limits of legalism . . . War has its rules, of course—but by those very rules our enemies in this war on terror are outlaws.

—David Frum and Richard Perle,
An End to Evil: How to Win the War on Terror

"When I woke up I didn't know where I was. I'd lost conscious-ness at the side of the container, but when I woke up I was in the middle—lying on top of dead bodies, breathing the stench of their blood and urine. They'd herded maybe 300 of us into each container, the type you get on ordinary lorries, packed in so tightly our knees were against our chests, and almost immediately we started to suffocate. We lived because someone made holes with a machine gun, though they were shooting low and still more died from the bullets. When we got out, about twenty in each container were still alive."

Asif Iqbal was describing his survival, together with his friends Ruhal Ahmed and Shafiq Rasul, after a massacre by U.S.-backed Northern Alliance forces in Afghanistan, at the start of their journey to Guantánamo Bay. We were speaking in a house in southern Britain in March 2004, four days after their release.

Their faces gaunt with accumulated stress and exhaustion, they spoke softly, still stunned by the change in their circumstances. "I just can't believe we're sitting here," Ahmed said. "This time last week, we were in the cages at Guantánamo."

Detained at Gitmo from almost the beginning, Iqbal and Rasul were among the first prisoners to be named. (Their friend Ahmed arrived in Cuba almost a month after them, on February 10, 2002.) A stream of reporters had been to their homes in Tipton, near Birmingham in the west Midlands, trying to ascertain what it was about its apparently nondescript Muslim community that had spawned, at least in Donald Rumsfeld's eyes, three deadly terrorists. They found few clues. Rasul was described as an indifferent Muslim, fond of trendy designer clothes, whose family found it difficult to persuade him to attend the mosque. "As far as I'm concerned, these are three safe guys who I used to play football with," Ala Uddin, the president of a local soccer team, told *The New York Times.* "I find it astonishing that they are under arrest, suspected of being terrorists."

For more than two years, attorneys instructed by the families of Rasul and Iqbal fought a dogged legal battle, arguing that the reasons for their detention should be reviewed by the American federal courts. Until a short time before their release, the two men remained unaware of it, although by then the case had been set down for argument in the U.S. Supreme Court. In June 2004, the court ruled in their favor. It is hard to believe that any court operating under recognizable standards of due process would have found their incarceration justified. As the authorities on both sides of the Atlantic were eventually forced to concede, there was no evidence that they ever carried arms, and they were not captured on any battlefield. For months in the summer of

2003, Gitmo's interrogators sought to prove they had been to an al-Qaeda terrorist training camp, and accused them of having met Osama bin Laden and Mohamed Atta, the leader of the 9/11 hijackers. Finally, it was the British Security Service, MI5, that came up with documentary proof that these allegations were false.

The three men came home: In that sense they were lucky. But while others, apparently as innocent of involvement in terrorism, are still at Guantánamo, their experiences were typical in two significant ways: the privation and brutality they endured from their captors in Afghanistan, and for the blundering imprecision of the process by which they were "screened," and hence dispatched to Cuba.

Rasul, twenty-six at the time of his release, Ahmed, twenty-two, and Iqbal, also twenty-two, were boyhood friends. They traveled to Pakistan in early September 2001, before the marriage Iqbal's parents had arranged for him to a woman in Faisalabad. Ahmed was to be best man; Rasul hoped to do a computer course in Pakistan after the wedding because the fees were lower there than in England. None of them, according to their families and former Tipton neighbors, was in any sense a fundamentalist: Their brand of Islam was never that of the Taliban. They did not, for example, wear beards; they liked soccer, and had Christian friends. But like many young Muslims in Pakistan in the fall of 2001, they crossed the border into Afghanistan in October 2001, as it became clear that one of the world's poorest countries was about to be attacked. Their plan was to render humanitarian aid, using the money they had saved for their trip.

They were, certainly, naïve. But as the bombing began and realization dawned of the extent to which they were out of their depth, they tried to escape: They were potential targets not only for U.S. warplanes, but the Taliban, for whom their lack of facial hair made them dangerously visible. Trying to avoid the advancing front, yet unaware exactly where it was, they found themselves in the city of Kunduz, which was promptly surrounded and bombarded by General Rashid Dostum's troops. Together with thousands of the city's inhabitants, they left on a convoy of trucks. Their own vehicle was shelled, killing almost everyone on board. "We were trapped," Iqbal said. "There was nothing we could do but give ourselves up. They took our money, our shoes, all our warm clothes, and put us in lines."

They found themselves part of a vast column of prisoners. Rasul said: "You'd look down the slope and there were lines and lines of people, as far as the eye could see. We went through the mountains and the open desert. There were these massive ditches full of bodies. We thought this was the end. We thought they were going to kill us all." Many of the prisoners were wounded and died by the wayside. Their account of these events closely matches testimony from other witnesses and the conclusions drawn by human rights groups. John Heffernan of Physicians for Human Rights went to the area through which the Tipton three were marched a few months later: "The whereabouts of many taken captive remained unknown. We traveled down the road a few miles into the desert. We smelled the unmistakable odor of decaying flesh and soon found bulldozer tracks and skeletal remains."

After two days, they were part of a huge group of prisoners crammed into truck containers, lined up in a row. It was night, Iqbal said, and what was now turning into a massacre began under the glare of spotlights, which he claimed were operated by

American special forces troops. "The last thing I remember is that it got really hot, and everyone started screaming and banging. It was like someone had lit a fire beneath the containers. You could feel the moisture running off your body, and people were ripping off their clothes." When he came to, he had not drunk for more than two days. Maddened by thirst, he wiped the streaming walls with a cloth and sucked out the moisture, until he realized he was drinking the bodily fluids of the massacred prisoners. "We were like zombies. We stank, we were covered in blood and the smell of death."

Freed from the trucks, they were taken into Dostum's Shebargan prison, where they were held in appalling conditions for the next month. Most of the buildings were open to the elements, and often it snowed. To make room inside its bare communal cells, the prisoners lay down in four-hour shifts. They were fed a quarter of a *naan* bread each day, with a small cup of water: sometimes, said Rasul, there were fights over the rations. "There were people with horrific injuries—limbs that had been shot off—and nothing was done," Rasul said. "I'll never forget one Arab who was missing half his jaw. For ten days until his death he was screaming and crying continuously, begging to be killed."

A few days earlier Taliban prisoners had organized the uprising against their captors at Qala-i-Jhangi Fort at Mazar-e-Sharif, and western reporters paid a visit to Shebargan. They seemed blind to the misery there, Rasul said. "All they seemed to be interested in was if any of us knew the American Taliban John Walker Lindh."

Another visitor was John Heffernan. Again, he corroborated the Tipton three's story. "There were nearly 3,000 of them being held in squalid conditions at Shebargan under the control of Dostum, whose palatial headquarters were across the street." His colleague, the forensic anthropologist William Haglund, who had earlier led investigations of mass graves in Bosnia, Rwanda, Sri Lanka and Sierra Leone, went back to Shebargan under United Nations auspices a few months later. By chance, on the day he arrived, Dostum had gone into the mountains, leaving behind a military escort that allowed him to visit and open a grave. "I uncovered one small corner, exposing fifteen remains which were quite complete, and did autopsies on three, chosen at random. There were no signs of trauma and these were all young men. This is consistent with death by asphyxiation. I told Dostum's security chief who was standing there that they had died from suffocation, and there was this big silence hanging over the desert."

Haglund also found eyewitnesses who told how the prisoners had been driven into the trucks, while Dostum's men tried to keep local people away. "The whole experience hearkened back to Bosnia for me—suddenly they were like cats in a sandbox, trying to hide the traces of what they had done." It was impossible to say how many bodies the grave might contain, he said, but it could run into thousands. Haglund and Heffernan pressed the U.S. government to provide backing and the necessary security for a full investigation into the mass grave. The White House initially promised support, but after the spring of 2002, Heffernan said, the Pentagon and State Department simply "stonewalled." Some witnesses had repeated the claim by the Tipton men that U.S. Special Forces looked on as the massacre began, he added, but these reports were unconfirmed. The Pentagon has denied them. "Allowing a full inquiry would be in America's interest too," he said. "If we have nothing to hide, it will dispel the claims and suspicions."

Ten days after the three men's arrival at Shebargan, the International Red Cross paid a visit, bringing some improvement and an increase in the water supply. But by now all three were malnourished and suffering from amoebic dysentery. Ahmed said: "We were covered with lice. All day long you were scratching, scratching. I was bleeding from my chest, my head." Iqbal added: "We lost so much weight that if I stood up I could carry water in the gap between my collarbone and my flesh." Prisoners died daily. All this time they could see American troops on the other side of the gates.

After a month of this living hell, on December 27 or 28, the Red Cross spoke to the three and promised they would contact the British Embassy in Islamabad and ask them to intervene on their behalf. Instead, as soon as they realized they were British, Dostum's troops put them in chains, marched them through the main gate of the prison, and handed them over to the American special forces. Like most prisoners in Afghanistan, they were immediately hooded. Ahmed said: "They put something like a sandbag over my head so you could see nothing. Then we got thrown on to a truck. They taped the sacks at the bottom of our necks, making it difficult to breathe." Casual brutality, the three men said, was now the norm. The Americans took them to Shebargan airport, where they were beaten, then loaded on a plane. "I wanted to use the toilet," Rasul said. "Someone smacked me on the back of my head with his gun. I started peeing myself."

Trussed like chickens, their chains replaced by plastic ties, they were flown to the U.S. detention center at Kandahar. The weather was freezing. Wearing only thin *salwar kameez,* with no socks or shoes, they were tied together with a rope and led into the camp, where they waited to be processed. In the very different setting of a sitting room in suburban England, Iqbal demonstrated how they were made to kneel, bent double, with their foreheads touching the ground: "If your head wasn't touching the floor or you let it rise up a little they put their boots on the back of your neck and forced it down. We were kept like that for two or three hours." According to Rasul, "I lifted up my head slightly because I was really in pain. The sergeant came up behind me, kicked my legs from underneath me, then knelt on my back. They took me outside and searched me while one man was sitting on me, kicking and punching."

All this time they were still wearing their hoods. Then one soldier took a Stanley knife and cut off their clothes. Naked and freezing, they were made to squat while the soldiers searched their bodily cavities and photographed them. At last, they said, they were frog-marched through a barbed-wire maze and put into a half-open tent where they were told to dress in blue prison overalls. They had not washed since the container massacre a month earlier. There, Iqbal had sustained a ricochet wound to the elbow. Displaying an ugly purple scar, he said that by the time he reached Kandahar, it had become infected. Violence against detainees at Kandahar appeared to be casual and routine. In repeated "shakedown" searches of the sleeping tents, copies of the Koran were trampled on by soldiers and, on one occasion, they said, thrown into a toilet bucket. On many nights, the guards carried out head-counts every hour to keep the prisoners awake.

It was late at night on the day of their arrival by the time they had been processed, but next morning, they were taken straight to their first interrogation. Rasul said: "A special forces guy sat there holding a gun to my temple, a 9mm pistol. He said if I made any movement he'd blow my head off." Each endured several such sessions at Kandahar: Each time, they said, they were questioned on their knees, in chains, always at gunpoint. Often they were kicked or beaten. Not all their interrogators were American. Iqbal and Rasul also described an English officer in a maroon beret who said he was a member of Britain's special forces regiment, the Special Air Service. "He had a posh English accent," Rasul said. "He mentioned the names of British prisons and said we'd end up there." Iqbal said the S.A.S. officer told him: "Don't worry, you won't be beaten today because you're with me." Ahmed said he was also questioned by an officer from MI5. "All the time I was kneeling with a guy standing on the backs of my legs and another holding a gun to my head. The MI5 man says: 'I'm from the U.K., I'm from MI5, and I've got some questions for you.' He says he was called Dave. He told me: 'We've got your names, we've got your passports, we know you've been funded by an extremist group, and we know you've been to this mosque in Birmingham. We've got photos of you.'" None of this was true.

A senior officer from special forces, who served in Afghanistan attached to a unit that worked with the CIA, told me there was nothing he found implausible, or indeed surprising, about the three Tipton men's account of Kandahar. It was, he said, just the way things had been done there. "After 9/11, few thought it wrong to slap these guys around." From the very different perspective of Human Rights Watch, John Sifton, who has interviewed numerous freed prisoners from Gitmo and Afghanistan, also confirmed the Tipton men's credibility. "Their descriptions of violent treatment and abusive interrogations at Kandahar are completely consistent with testimony we have gathered from scores of detainees who were held both there and at Bagram, near Kabul."

However, tough conditions and physical abuse were not the only flaws in the U.S. process that saw hundreds of prisoners flown from Afghanistan to Gitmo. As a means of separating terrorist wheat from footsoldier chaff, it was surprisingly defective.

One freezing day in January 2004, I found myself at the Pentagon, interviewing a top-level official, who worked closely with Rumsfeld, about the occupation of Iraq. He was palpably wary, and in almost an hour said nothing much illuminating. As an afterthought, I asked him why, of all the places in the world, America had chosen its tiny enclave in Cuba—a remote and seemingly inconvenient location—to lock up detainees. (Gitmo was seized on an "indefinite lease" in 1903, as one of the spoils of the Spanish-American war. It is still impossible for U.S. planes to overfly Communist Cuba, necessitating a long and awkward dogleg: As a result, the regular flights to Gitmo from Jacksonville, Florida, take almost three hours.) For a moment, relieved to be off the subject of Iraq, the official dropped his guard. "Because the legal advice was we could do what we wanted to them there," he said. "They were going to be outside any court's jurisdiction."

From the moment the Guantánamo detention camp was first conceived at the Pentagon in December 2001, its most salient feature was that Gitmo and its prisoners would be outside all known mechanisms of American and international law. As a French detainee, Nizar Sassi, put it in a postcard to his family, which somehow eluded the military censor, "If you want a definition of this place, you don't have the right to have rights." Through the fall of 2001 and the first days of 2002, a large and bold legal idea was taking shape in the collective mind of the Bush administration. It sprang from the judgment, reached in less than twenty-four hours after 9/11, that the attacks on New York and Washington could not be treated as matters for law enforcement agencies, but as acts of war. But this was a war unlike any other, being fought not against some discrete and visible foe, but an amorphous, global enemy: "terror." In the opinion of the lawyers at the Department of Justice and the Pentagon, it needed new rules, and Bush and his administration considered it their duty to compose them.

The law of war had always "evolved" in response to events, they argued, in an attempt to minimize their radicalism: It usually amounted to a *post hoc* codification of messy, contingent events. At the same time, they regarded the laws agreed between states as more malleable, as somehow less sacrosanct, than those enacted by national bodies such as the U.S. Congress. For them the phrase "victor's justice" carried no pejorative meaning, but simply reflected a world view attuned to the nuances of power and *realpolitik*. One of Rumsfeld's key advisors, the lawyer and marine Lieutenant Colonel William Lietzau, quoted an aphorism by the German jurist Hersch Lauterpacht: "If international law is, in some ways, at the vanishing point of law, the law of war is, even more conspicuously, at the vanishing point of international law." And, Lietzau continued in a paper he gave at Harvard in August 2002, "one could add the observation that if the law of war is at the vanishing point of international law, the war with al-Qaeda and, more broadly, the global war on terrorism raise issues that are at the vanishing point of the law of war." The war with al-Qaeda, he went on, was unlike any previous conflict, and America was fighting it not against a state, but against "nebulous networks of secret cells—not found on maps—with no capitals to destroy."

The consequences of this analysis first surfaced on November 13, 2001, when Bush, acting in his capacity as commander in chief of the armed services, issued a Presidential Military Order declaring that captured al-Qaeda terrorists could be tried by special military commissions, free of the restrictions imposed by the civilian courts. Captives who merited such treatment would not, he made clear, be treated as prisoners of war but "unlawful combatants." Then, however, it appeared that the scope of this definition would be limited to big-time terrorists. "Non-U.S. citizens who plan and/or commit mass murder are more than criminal suspects," Bush said. "They are unlawful combatants who seek to destroy our country and our way of life." Vice President Dick Cheney even suggested that the term "unlawful combatant" might only apply to terrorists captured on American soil: "The basic proposition here is that somebody who comes into the United States of America illegally, who conducts a terrorist operation killing thousands of innocent Americans—men, women and children—is not a lawful combatant. They don't deserve to be treated as a prisoner of war." The last time this happened was when six German would-be saboteurs were captured inside America during the Second World War. Five of them (all but the Nazi agent who eventually, after repeated unsuccessful attempts, managed to convince the FBI that he and his cohorts were not fantasists) were executed.

Under the terms of Bush's order, it would be the President alone who had the power to decide to whom this "unlawful combatant" definition would be applied. By the time Camp X-ray opened two months later, the concept of who such a person might be had changed and expanded beyond recognition. It now meant not just someone thought to have engaged directly in terrorism against America, but anyone captured in Afghanistan suspected of fighting with the Taliban—a very different thing. In order to justify this, the administration was effectively taking the position that the Taliban and al-Qaeda were one and the same, and that involvement in what had been an Afghan civil war linked a fighter indelibly with the events of 9/11—hence the fearsome rhetoric from Bush and his colleagues quoted above. But this analysis was very questionable. Although the Taliban leader Mullah Omar had invited Osama bin Laden to return to Afghanistan in 1996, the overlap between his organization and al-Qaeda was extremely small. According to one senior U.S. intelligence official who is still investigating the matter, "in 1996 it was non-existent, and by 2001, no more than 50 people."

The consequence for prisoners taken in Afghanistan was that they would not be treated in accordance with the third Geneva Convention of 1949, which had, in Lieutenant Colonel Lietzau's words, been "written for a different kind of war." At the end of a fierce little battle over the issue with the State Department, Alberto Gonzalez, the White House chief counsel, set out the general principles in his memorandum to President Bush on January 25, 2002: "The nature of the new war places a high premium on factors such as the ability to quickly obtain information from captured terrorists and their sponsors in order to avoid further atrocities against American civilians, and the need to try terrorists for war crimes such as wantonly killing civilians," he wrote. "In my judgment," Gonzalez went on, "this new paradigm renders obsolete Geneva's strict limitations on questioning of enemy prisoners and renders quaint some of its provisions."

Had the detainees been classed as enemy prisoners of war ("EPWs") under Geneva, their treatment both in Afghanistan and later at Gitmo would have been very different. With no obligation on prisoners to relate anything beyond their name, rank and number, the intensive and coercive interrogation that took place in both places would have been impossible. They would also have been entitled to confinement in barracks of a standard equivalent to their captors; the cages at Guantánamo would have been illegal. And had they been classed as EPWs captured in what the law of war calls the "international armed conflict" in Afghanistan, they would have long ago been released. The International Committee of the Red Cross used its power under the convention to declare this conflict over in February 2002. To continue holding 600 men against whom no charges had been filed for more than two-and-a-half years would have been impossible.

In fact, the Geneva Convention's rules do create scope in exceptional circumstances for prisoners to be deprived of its protections, and the U.S. military has long recognized this in its own standing orders. Captured warriors who do not display uniforms, badges of rank or other insignia, or belong to a recognizable military command structure can be held not to merit EPW status, and it is certainly arguable that this could apply to a member of al-Qaeda. However, under both the Convention and U.S. procedures going back decades, there has to be a full legal hearing to determine the facts in every prisoner's case. There is no recent precedent for classifying a huge group of men as unlawful combatants by executive fiat. In the 1991 Gulf War the U.S. military held 1,196 such hearings. In almost 75 percent of them the prisoners were found to be innocent civilians and freed.

The Pentagon's Central Command, whose area of responsibility includes both Afghanistan and Iraq, had updated its own rules as recently as February 1995, when it issued Regulation 27-13 to all personnel. Entitled "Captured Persons: Determination of Eligibility for Enemy Prisoner of War Status," it says "Any person who has committed a belligerent act . . . will be treated as an EPW unless a competent Tribunal [so] determines." At this tribunal, the prisoner must have an interpreter "who shall be competent in English and Arabic (or other language understood by the detainee)." It must be chaired by a military lawyer, and its proceedings must be recorded. Witnesses must testify under oath. (Helpfully, says the regulation, "a form for Muslim witnesses is attached.") The detainee has the right to be present, to cross-examine witnesses, and to look at documents, although classified sections may be concealed. As for the verdict, unless the evidence proves he does not deserve it, the prisoner must be given full EPW status. In which case: good-bye, Guantánamo Bay.

Secretary of State Colin Powell argued forcefully that to disregard this provision had serious drawbacks. To deny detainees hearings and decide that all of them, "across the board," lay outside the scope of Geneva would "reverse over a century of U.S. policy . . . and undermine the protections of the law of war for our troops, both in this specific context and in general," he wrote on January 26, 2002, to Bush's chief counsel Gonzalez and his national security advisor, Condoleezza Rice. It would also undermine support from America's allies, especially in Europe, who might henceforth be reluctant to cooperate in "bringing terrorists to justice."

Internal Gitmo documents I have obtained make clear that even as Powell was writing, the soldiers of the Joint Task Force assumed that there *would* be individual tribunals to determine the status of every prisoner. Toward the end of January, Lieutenant Colonel T. L. Miller, the task force military lawyer, drew up a memorandum that described both the normal position under international law and the way tribunals should be organized under CENTCOM's regulation. Its language and approach suggest that he had not even begun to consider the possibility that tribunals would not be held at all: His memo's purpose, he wrote, was simply to "determine the requirements for . . . tribunals under Geneva Convention III." His "issues" for consideration were practical ones: "Where's the relevant evidence? . . . If a detainee is found to be an EPW, what Geneva Convention protections does he get that he's not receiving now? How will that affect force protection and security?" Finally, concerned that the number of prisoners was rapidly mounting and that giving them all their due Geneva process might take a long time, Miller asked: "Is one standing tribunal panel enough? To get a feel for how long it will take one tribunal to dispose of a single case, think of an administrative discharge board. An admin board might complete two cases in one day."

Miller, however, was not making policy. Bush and Rumsfeld were. On January 28, Rumsfeld visited Guantánamo and declared "There is no ambiguity in this case. They are not POWs. They will not be determined to be POWs." Next day, Bush told reporters that the detainees were "killers," who would not be granted the status of prisoners of war. His formal ruling came on February 7, 2002, with a "presidential determination of legal status of detainees." Citing what he called his "authority under the Constitution," Bush said that none of them, whatever the circumstances of the capture, would count as EPWs. Although other aspects of the Geneva treaties—such as the ban on the rape and pillage of civilians—did apply to the Afghan war, the Convention would cover neither al-Qaeda nor Taliban prisoners. The Taliban did not qualify as a regular army that met Geneva's requirements, and there was therefore no need for tribunals. In the words of one Pentagon lawyer, "Bush had cut CENTCOM's own legal guys off at the knees." All the prisoners were now to be deemed unlawful combatants and denied normal protections because President Bush had said so.

Bush's decision was derived from the claim, first set out in a memorandum in early January by John Yoo, a deputy assistant Attorney General, that Taliban-controlled Afghanistan was a "failed state," whose "territory had been largely overrun and held by violence by a militia or faction rather than by a government." On that basis, Yoo argued, none of the Taliban armed forces met the criteria of having chains of command, uniforms or insignia required for protection from Geneva. Yoo's proposition was later endorsed by a further memo from Attorney General John Ashcroft, but it was, at best, dubious. In fact, by 2001 the Taliban controlled all but a fragment of Afghanistan's far north, and while they did not wear western-style uniforms, Taliban soldiers were distinguished by black turbans, and—like any effective fighting force—conformed to a strict hierarchy of command.

Moreover, Bush's determination was not merely unilateral. It was, according to the plain and ordinary meaning of the Geneva Convention itself, illegal. Even if it could be shown that the Taliban were not meeting their own obligations under Geneva, this did not give Bush the right to repudiate the Convention himself. Article 142 of the Third Convention says that its signatories, including America, do have the right to "denounce" it. But they may do so only after giving one year's notice in writing to the Swiss Federal Council, and if a state happens to be involved in a conflict at the time, its repudiation "shall not take effect until peace has been concluded." While a war continues, it is still bound by "the obligations which the parties to the conflict are bound to fulfill by virtue of the principles of the law of nations."

Bush may have been acting lawfully in respect to the U.S. Constitution. But as an opinion issued in July 2004 for the International Bar Association by Vaughan Lowe, Oxford's professor of international law, and the humanitarian lawyer Guy Goodwin-Gill states, his decisions about prisoners were "manifestly incompatible with international law . . . [Bush's] argument also ignores the fundamental principle of international humanitarian law, namely that the obligation to abide by the rules does *not* depend on reciprocity, and that the rules exist to protect certain classes of individuals, not just the interests of states."

As the argument raged in Washington, Colin Powell extracted just one, utterly meaningless concession. It was summarized by a phrase Rumsfeld was to use time and again—the detainees might not be EPWs, but they were being treated in ways "consistent with the principles" of the Geneva Convention. (Bush sometimes put it another way: their treatment at Gitmo "adhered to its spirit.") Rumsfeld even claimed that all this was but a bureaucratic detail, and their precise legal status would have "no impact" on detainees' lives. "We will continue to treat them consistent with the principles of fairness, freedom and justice that our nation was founded on, the principles that they obviously abhor and which they sought to attack and destroy. Notwithstanding the isolated pockets of international hyperventilation, we do not treat detainees in any manner other than a manner that is humane."

It was only at the end of June 2004, when the White House published a series of formerly classified documents about Gitmo, that the depths of the hypocrisy that these claims concealed became apparent. For public consumption, Bush and Rumsfeld were saying that detainees' treatment would be consistent with the principles of Geneva. Indeed, even the classified text of Bush's February 7, 2002, determination began with the usual huffing and puffing about respecting prisoners' rights: "Our values as a nation . . . call for us to treat detainees humanely, including those who are not legally entitled to such treatment. Our nation has been and will continue to be a strong supporter of Geneva and its principles." But only, the secret version of the order went on, when this happened to suit America. "As a matter of policy, the United States Armed Forces shall continue to treat detainees humanely *and, to the extent appropriate and consistent with military necessity,* in a manner consistent with the principles of Geneva." [My italics.] If the commander in chief decided he had to breach even the elusive "spirit" of Geneva because he believed it necessary, he would feel free to do so.

Confident as Bush and Rumsfeld always sounded, they and their colleagues were fully aware of the novelty of what they were doing, and the danger of exposing it to legal challenge. Hence the comment of the Pentagon official I interviewed in January 2004: The beauty of Guantánamo, the administration believed, was that it was beyond the law. As the English Court of Appeal put it in the case of a British detainee whose family filed suit in a desperate attempt to persuade his government to exert the necessary diplomatic pressure to get him out, Gitmo existed in a "legal black hole." (This suit, organized by the British human-rights lawyer Louise Christian, did have the effect of forcing the UK government to press, at least in public, for the detainees' release.)

A fuller exposition was set out by Colonel Dan F. McCallum of the Pentagon's training and doctrine command, who presented a paper on the choice of Gitmo at the Army National War College in Washington in March 2003. He had interviewed officials from every important agency involved, including the CIA, the Department of Defense, the State Department and the Department of Justice. Rumsfeld, he began, had described Guantánamo as "the least worst place we could have selected." In fact, said McCallum, it was a great deal better than that.

In making its choice, the administration had considered four possible options: a foreign country, the U.S., some other American territory, and Guantánamo. America was ruled out by the danger of a prison camp attracting terrorist attacks, while holding detainees abroad might make it difficult for U.S. intelligence officers to get access to them. When it came to a choice between Gitmo and some other remote U.S. possession, the government's lawyers believed Gitmo had one enormous advantage. Other territories, McCallum wrote, were "within the jurisdiction of the federal courts." That meant that any detainee who wished to challenge an aspect of his treatment, his denial of Geneva rights, or his continued incarceration, could have brought a federal habeas corpus action, the "judicial review of the detention of a person to determine if the detention is lawful." At Gitmo, the Department of Justice (DoJ) believed, there was no such risk. As the administration was later to argue in the case that made its way to the Supreme Court, sovereignty over Gitmo still belonged to Cuba, despite the indefinite U.S. lease, and therefore foreign citizens held there could not bring cases to American courts.

"Gitmo is a unique piece of property, owned by Cuba but controlled by the U.S. under a perpetual lease," Colonel McCallum gushed. "It minimized foreign relations concerns and domestic security concerns ... since the property belonged to Cuba, DoJ assessed the litigation risk as minimal." Far from being the least worst place, "Gitmo was the best possible place."

Meanwhile, the effect of the administration's decisions was simply to remove all possible scrutiny from the process of determining prisoners' status. Instead of being tested by a tribunal, it was enough for evidence merely to be asserted that an individual was a Taliban fighter or a member of al-Qaeda, and he would be on his way to Gitmo. In the statements made by administration officials and their prominent supporters, such as Professor Ruth Wedgwood of Johns Hopkins University, evaluation was replaced by tautology. If you were in Guantánamo, it was because you had been "captured on the battlefield," and if you had been captured on the battlefield, you must have been with the Taliban or al-Qaeda. Entirely missing was any attempt to ascertain, in the cases of each prisoner, whether any of these claims were true.

I interviewed Lieutenant Colonel Lietzau, Rumsfeld's former advisor, at the Pentagon. First I asked him about the insurgents and Baathist irregulars in Iraq, the men responsible for the continuing mayhem of suicide bombings and attacks on coalition troops. They seemed just as unlawful as anyone at Gitmo in their attitude to combat and did not appear to wear insignia or be part of any structure of command; some might well be members of al-Qaeda. Yet all were being treated as enemy prisoners of war and given—at least in theory—their Geneva rights. "It's a great question," Lietzau said. "It's disturbing. I don't know the answer. One of the things that upsets me is the lack of consistency." Then I asked him why he was sure there was no need to hold tribunals at Guantánamo. His answer was breathtaking. "It doesn't make much sense in this situation because there aren't really any factual disputes. No one is saying, 'Well wait a second. I wasn't part of the Taliban.' "

In this, he was mistaken.

In a written media briefing in early 2002, in an attempt to dampen criticism of conditions at Camp X-ray, the White House stated: "Some treatment conditions are not compatible with the extraordinary security risk posed by these detainees, who are extremely violent and dangerous and pose a threat to the U.S. forces who are guarding them and to each other." Yet since then, more than 150 of them have been released. Of these just five, according to intelligence officials cited by *The New York Times,* have gone on to commit acts of violence against U.S. forces or anyone else. A senior Pentagon intelligence analyst told me he found this surprising: "Quite frankly, I'd have thought that if they weren't terrorists before they went to Gitmo, they would have been by the time they came out," he said without irony. Many of those who were released spent their entire time in Guantánamo making the exact claim that Lietzau said was never an issue: "Wait a second. I wasn't part of the Taliban." It had often taken two years or more for their protestations to be believed.

Another freed British detainee is Tarek Dergoul from east London. When I met him in May 2004, the effects of his ordeal were very visible. A slight, slim man, he had difficulty walking: for weeks, his American captors in Afghanistan failed to treat his frosbitten feet until a big toe turned gangrenous and had to be amputated. He also lost most of his left arm, the result of a shrapnel wound. Two months after regaining his freedom, he was still having nightmares and flashbacks, especially of his many beatings, and was about to begin treatment at the Medical Foundation for the Care of Victims of Torture. "I get migraines, I'm depressed, and I suffer from memory loss. There's stuff that happened embedded in my head that I can't remember."

Born to Moroccan parents in Mile End in December 1977, Dergoul was once in trouble for stealing a computer chip, for which he was sentenced to community service. After leaving school at fifteen, he worked in a succession of jobs: selling double glazing, office cleaning, driving a minicab, and working as a carer at an old people's home in Suffolk. Living in east London, many of his friends were from Pakistan, and he decided to visit the country for an extended holiday in July 2001. "Before I went, I'd never even heard of Osama bin Laden or the Taliban, and I didn't know where Afghanistan was," he said. "I wasn't political and I didn't read the papers. My parents are religious, but personally, I never went to the Mosque."

After the September 11 attacks, he and two Pakistani friends had an idea for what, in hindsight, was one of the worst-judged business ventures of all time. Dergoul had £5,000 in cash, which he pooled with his friends' savings. "The plan was to buy some property away from where the bombing was. We thought we could buy it very cheap, then sell it at a profit after the war." They traveled to Jalalabad and looked at several empty homes. On the verge of signing a deal, Dergoul and his friends spent the night in an empty villa. While they were asleep, a bomb landed on it, killing his friends. He went outside, only to be hit by the blast from another projectile. For at least a week, wounded and unable to walk, he lay among the ruins, drinking from a tap that still worked and living on biscuits and raisins he had in his pocket. Exposed to the freezing weather, his toes turned black from frostbite.

At last he was found by troops loyal to the Northern Alliance. They treated him well, taking him to a hospital where he was given food and three operations on his arm. However, after five weeks, he was driven to an airfield and handed over to Americans who arrived by helicopter. Dergoul said the Americans paid a $5,000 bounty for him. Many of those he met at Gitmo had been "purchased" in the same way.

John Sifton, the researcher on Afghanistan at Human Rights Watch, told me that $5,000 was the standard fee paid by the United States for a "terrorist" suspect, and in his own interviews with former detainees in Afghanistan and Pakistan, he had found many examples. As supposed terrorists, he said, "they were all the most extreme cases of mistaken identity—simply the wrong guys: a farmer; a taxi driver and all his passengers; people with absolutely no connection with the Taliban or terrorism, who actually abhorred or fought against them." In addition to the victims of bounty hunters, there was another group of detainees denounced and captured after getting into business or land disputes, Sifton said, citing examples that amounted to little more than "land grabs." In many cases, after detainees were sent to Gitmo, their homes and other property were looted.

The Americans flew Dergoul to the U.S. detention camp at Bagram airbase near Kabul, where violence and sexual humiliation appeared to be routine. "When I arrived, with a bag over my head, I was stripped naked and taken to a big room with fifteen or twenty MPs [military police]. They started taking photos, and then they did a full cavity search. As they were doing that they were taking close-ups, concentrating on my private parts." Possibly because he was British, Dergoul said he was spared the beatings he saw being administered to others at Bagram. But in the neighboring cages, "guards with guns and baseball bats would make the detainees squat for hours, and if they fell over from exhaustion, they'd beat them until they lost consciousness. They called it 'beat down.' "

Dergoul's interrogators repeatedly accused him of having fought with al-Qaeda during bin Laden's last stand in the Tora Bora mountains. (It is possible that the Northern Alliance bounty hunters had made this claim in order to justify their fee.) At the time, he insisted, he had no idea of Tora Bora's significance and had never been there. But in the course of twenty to twenty-five interrogations at Bagram—including one session with a British team from MI5—he was told his family's assets would be seized unless he confessed, but if he did make admissions, he would be sent home. "I was in extreme pain from the frostbite and other injuries, and I was so weak I could barely stand. It was freezing cold and I was shaking and shivering like a washing machine. Finally I agreed I'd been at Tora Bora—though I still wouldn't admit I'd ever met bin Laden."

After about a month, in February 2002, Dergoul was taken south to another camp at Kandahar. His memories of this time are hazy: It was there that his feet, left untreated, went septic, and as the infection spread through his body, he underwent a further amputation. In three months there, he said, he had only two showers. Finally, on May 1, his head, beard and pubic hair were shaved, he was dressed in goggles and an orange jumpsuit, injected with a sedative, and flown to Guantánamo Bay.

The stories of prisoners still at Gitmo suggest the evidence they are "terrorists" is equally questionable, and many, like Dergoul, were captured far from any battlefield—in some cases, in countries that were not at war. Airat Vakhitov, one of eight Russians consigned to Gitmo, was originally captured not by the

Northern Alliance but the Taliban, who held him for seven months in a dark, stinking dungeon, subject to frequent beatings, on suspicion of working as a spy for the Russian intelligence service, the S.V.R. When the regime fell he was discovered there by a reporter for *Le Monde,* and he must have imagined he was on his way to freedom. Instead, he was picked up by the Americans and sent to Guantánamo Bay.

Moazzem Begg, a father of four (the youngest of whom he has never seen), lived in the British city of Birmingham. In 2001, he took his British wife Sally and the rest of the family to Afghanistan and opened an elementary school. Shortly after 9/11, fearful of the coming war, they fled to Pakistan. It was in its capital, Islamabad, that Begg was seized from the house the family was renting at 3 A.M. one night in January 2002. His captors failed to search him properly: Before reaching his destination, he was able to call his father in England on his cell phone, and he told him he had been captured by Americans and placed in the trunk of a car.

Begg's family, who deny he had any link with the Taliban or al-Qaeda, filed a habeas corpus suit with the Pakistani courts, where all the relevant government agencies denied on oath that he was their prisoner, saying they had no idea of his whereabouts. He was taken to Bagram, where he spent a year. Finally he arrived in Gitmo at the beginning of 2003.

His lawyer is a veteran civil rights attorney, Gareth Peirce. Her efforts once did much to expose several miscarriages of justice in another war on terror, Britain's struggle against the Irish Republican Army. "Begg was unlawfully seized, and that ought to be the beginning and end of his predicament," she said. Like other attorneys who seek to represent Gitmo detainees, she cannot even write to, much less meet, her prospective client. "There seems to be a new world order, an acceptance of utter illegality. You have all these wonderful treaties after World War Two—the Geneva Conventions, bans on torture—and all of them have been torn up. Effectively you are allowing international law to be re-written."

Wahhab and Bisher al-Rawi are brothers in their late thirties. Both were born in Iraq, but left for Britain as children, when their father was arrested and tortured by Saddam Hussein's security service. Wahhab, along with the rest of the family, took U.K. nationality. Bisher, however, kept his Iraqi citizenship. The family had abandoned valuable lands in Iraq and thought that if one of them remained Iraqi, it would be easier to reclaim their property when Saddam's regime came to an end.

In November 2002, the brothers and two other men, Jamil el-Banna, a Jordanian who had lived in Britain for twenty-five years, and Abdullah al-Janoudi, a British citizen, traveled to Gambia, the tiny strip of a state barely twenty miles wide on the west coast of Africa. They had come up with a novel business idea: a mobile plant to process Gambia's main crop, peanuts. By taking the plant to the farms, rather than shipping nuts to a central factory, they could cut costs and maximize profits. The four men had poured their savings into the project, and Wahhab al-Rawi had remortgaged his home. In all, they had raised close to $1 million.

Wahhab traveled first and, working through a local agent, spent most of the money on equipment, vehicles, an office and other items. When the other three arrived in Gambia's capital, Banjul, Wahhab was at the airport to meet them. There, however, all four men, plus the agent, were arrested by the local intelligence service. The agent was released after three days. As far as the out-side world was concerned, the al-Rawi brothers and their part-ners simply disappeared. "At the very first interrogation, it was just Gambians, and I showed them all the papers relating to the busi-ness," Wahhab al-Rawi said. "We were in this room at the Na-tional Intelligence Agency headquarters and this big American comes in. He said his name was Lee, and that he wanted to ask us some questions. He said it would take no more than four days."

Instead, for the next twenty-seven days, the four were moved around a series of safe houses in Banjul, interrogated regularly by Lee, other Americans and the Gambians: sometimes alone, and sometimes together. Al-Rawi said their interrogators claimed that they had been planning to set up a terrorist training camp in the Gambian countryside, using the expertise his brother Bisher had gained from his outdoor hobbies—diving and parachuting. It was, as Wahhab pointed out, an inherently improbable allegation. Gambia's biggest industry is tourism, fueled by western seekers of its tropical sun. It would not be an easy place to hide a training camp. Although an Islamic country, it also has a large Christian minority. "I cooperated: I gave them all the answers," Wahhab al-Rawi said. "Yet they really didn't seem to know what they wanted. At one session, they even asked if I was working for the British secret service."

There was no physical ill-treatment, he said, but Lee and his American colleagues sometimes made threats: "They said, 'We're here to protect you, without us here the Gambians could get away with murder.' But my father had been to hell and back under Saddam. It didn't impress me." Bisher al-Rawi, it appears, had met the London-based Islamic cleric, Abu Qatada, who was later detained without charge by the British government under its own post-9/11 terrorism legislation. But none of the four, Wahhab said, had any involvement with politics of any kind, let alone radical Islamic militancy: "My brother Bisher? He can't even spell it."

The men's families pressed the British government to intervene. It seems that for Wahhab and al-Janoudi, the two British citizens, some kind of representations were eventually made. But the British Foreign Office told Bisher's family that he was not their responsibility. They should approach the government of Iraq—despite the fact that the al-Rawis were refugees from its government, against which Britain and America were at that moment about to go to war. Wahhab al-Rawi and al-Janoudi were finally released and flown back to Britain. The other two men were shipped by the Americans to Bagram, and after another month, Guantánamo. "They'll have to release them one day, they've done nothing," Wahhab told me. Meanwhile, he and his partners are ruined. "All of it—everything we invested—has gone. We never got any of it back." Tarek Dergoul got to know Bisher at Gitmo. He told him, he said, that he was sure that he and his friends had been denounced as part of a scheme to steal their money and equipment.

Another six Gitmo detainees were captured by American agents in Bosnia, moments after claims that their Islamic charity was linked with terrorism had been dismissed by the Bosnian human rights court. The internal Gitmo timeline refers to this event, saying it was personally authorized by Donald Rumsfeld. Martin Mubanga, another British prisoner of African descent, was captured in Zambia under circumstances that remain mysterious.

Overall, says a Human Rights Watch report published in

November 2003, American personnel have "repeatedly arrested persons mistakenly, whose identities are not known to them, some of whom later turn out to be civilians unconnected with any terrorist . . . activities. Such people are, like all detainees, held incommunicado and indefinitely, and are released at the whim of U.S. officials."

Candid U.S. personnel will admit that the scale of this injustice, the sheer numbers of people held in the most rigorous conditions, interrogated time and time again and vilified in public, is staggering. On my own visit to Gitmo in October 2003, one guard told me that the impression he had from his time spent "behind the wire" was that many of the prisoners were not really terrorists at all, although his superiors always insisted they were. In his view, at least 200 of those held in the maximum security cellblocks were harmless. The verdict from a senior Pentagon official with extensive knowledge of Guantánamo was more critical. "At least two-thirds" of the 600 detainees held as of May 2004 could, he said, be released without hesitation immediately.

In June 2004, *The New York Times* published a long investigative article about Gitmo, disclosing that the CIA had carried out a top-secret study of the detainees in September 2002. It concluded that "many of the accused terrorists appeared to be low-level recruits who went to Afghanistan to support the Taliban or even innocent men swept up in the chaos of the war." According to *The Times,* numerous officials who had seen the assessment said that "only a relative handful—some put the number at about a dozen, others more than two dozen—were sworn al-Qaeda members or other militants able to elucidate the organization's inner workings." Of these, not one was a leader or "senior operative."

★   ★   ★

Major John Smith, a military lawyer and one of the Pentagon's Gitmo media spokesmen, amplified Lieutenant Colonel Lietzau's assertion that there had never been a need to hold tribunals to determine the facts in every detainee's case. The reason, he said, was the "quite extensive screening process" America had in operation. Rumsfeld and Cheney have made similar claims. In Afghanistan, Smith said, "we've detained more than 8,000 individuals, most of whom have been screened and then further detention was determined not to be appropriate or necessary. The ones who are at Guantánamo right now were deemed in the country to be of special interest. They were taken out of the zone of operations, and they're continuously evaluated down there." In his view, this purely bureaucratic, administrative system was sufficient to prevent injustice.

Others disagree. Lieutenant Colonel Anthony Christino III formally retired from the U.S. Army on June 1, 2004, after a twenty-year career in Military Intelligence. One of his last assignments was at the heart of the Pentagon's war on terror as a senior watch officer for the central unit known as Joint Intelligence Task Force-Combating Terrorism (JITF-CT). When on shift, he was, he said, responsible for everything that went in or out of JITF-CT, including "analysis of critical, time-sensitive intelligence" about possible imminent attacks. Such intelligence would presumably have included information derived from interrogations conducted at Guantánamo. In his previous assignment in Germany, one of his roles had been to provide staff oversight of intelligence screening and interrogation operations throughout the Balkans, particularly in Kosovo. He also played a key role in coordinating intelligence support to army units in Afghanistan and at Guantánamo. In Christino's view, the screening process in Afghanistan was "flawed from the get-go."

Christino, who also holds a designation as an army historian, told me that these shortcomings have deep historical roots. After the Vietnam War, the U.S. Army had for decades neglected HUMINT—the gathering of intelligence from human sources—and the related craft of interrogating prisoners. Instead, it had placed overwhelming emphasis on an operational concept known as CEWI-Combat Electronic Warfare Intelligence. Military Intelligence personnel were spending their time analyzing communications intercepts and poring over photographic images taken by aircraft and satellites, not in learning how to build a rapport with a captured prisoner, and then, if he started to talk, how to figure out if he was telling the truth. "We became over-enamored with technology and failed to teach people skills." As someone who chose to specialize in counterintelligence and HUMINT, Christino said, he had been viewed as "opting out of the mainstream." Early in his career, he had even been warned by a friendly superior officer that focusing on these intelligence disciplines could result in "career suicide."

It is not commonly recognized, Christino said, that there are now simply *no* military intelligence personnel of officer rank in the U.S. Army who specialize in interrogation, as there were during the Vietnam War and earlier. Today, this crucial job is left to warrant officers (interrogation technicians) and enlisted soldiers (interrogators). Only a handful of Military Intelligence officers have been given any HUMINT training at all, and this will not have included much on interrogation.

Of course, the war on terror created a sudden resurgence in demand for these skills. According to Christino, however, by 2001 all the U.S. Army's most talented chief warrant officers and senior NCOs, who had honed their techniques in Vietnam and during the latter part of the Cold War, had retired. What was left, he said, was a generation who had learned sloppy methods in the Balkans, Haiti and Somalia, because they did not have the benefit of experienced senior leadership. "When any mid-level officer who had developed counterintelligence and/or HUMINT expertise tried to exert some leadership, they were simply pushed out of the way by more senior officers steeped in CEWI."

It was no surprise to Christino that in Afghanistan, as one internal Pentagon "after-action" report noted, the U.S. Army "got a wake-up call." The military intelligence soldiers who went there were "far too poorly trained" to identify real terrorists from the ordinary Taliban militia. Many of the Military Intelligence soldiers, in their late teens and early twenties, were "fresh out of Fort Huachuca," the Military Intelligence training school in Arizona, Christino said. To be accepted, they would have had to have graduated from high school and scored very well on the U.S. Army's entry tests. But following no more than sixteen weeks of specialized training, of which at most half might be spent on interrogation, they were let loose on prisoners such as Asif Iqbal and Tarek Dergoul. How good could a young soldier get in that time? "Not very," Christino said. "These kids—as bright and as dedicated to their mission as they may be—lack meaningful life, let alone professional, experiences. Contrast them with their law enforcement counterparts: a police officer will typically have an associates or bachelors degree in criminal justice and spend three to five years doing routine police work before he or she can even apply to become a detective. The army should require a similar degree of seasoning before an MI soldier becomes a HUMINT specialist responsible for screening or interrogation."

Worse, they were dealing with prisoners from the far side of a deep cultural gulf and were almost entirely reliant on interpreters, most of them contracted by private corporations. Their quality, said Christino, was often abysmal. A 2003 Pentagon report by Colonel Lawrence H. Saul, director of a military evaluation unit called the Center for Army Lessons Learned, supports that view. In both Iraq and Afghanistan, it states, "the lack of competent interpreters throughout the theater impeded operations . . . Bottom line, the U.S. Army does not have a fraction of the linguists required to operate in the Central Command (CENTCOM) area of responsibility. We have to rely on contract linguists for Dari, Pashtun and the numerous dialects of Arabic . . . laugh if you will, but many of the linguists with which I conversed were convenience store workers and cab drivers. None had any previous military experience. Most military linguists working in Iraq and Afghanistan only possess, on the average, a 2/2 Forces Command rating—which basically gives them the ability to tell the difference between a burro and a burrito."

Christino said the screeners' inexperience and difficulty in understanding what their prisoners were saying was exacerbated by another factor in Afghanistan. As so many freed detainees have claimed, "initially very few detainees were captured as a result of combat with U.S. troops on the battlefield. Almost all of them were turned over by the Northern Alliance, Pakistani troops, or others who perceived they might get some benefit from doing so. In a generic sense, they were selling their captives to the U.S. Army, and they came with what amounted to a sales pitch—a story to convince our troops that these people were valuable. Their story could be true; it could be fiction, or a combination of the two. The problem was that with inadequate training, little experience, and poor translation, our MI soldiers were largely incapable of discerning the difference."

Most Military Intelligence soldiers were, Christino said, motivated by an honest desire to do the right thing, to "make a contribution" after 9/11. But for an innocent detainee, this might have disastrous consequences. "Imagine: A Northern Alliance leader tells you this man is an Arab who was in a terrorist training camp—you want to believe it, and you don't want to take the risk of letting someone dangerous go. In another scenario, if you had information that someone frequently visited a mosque with an established connection to al-Qaeda, how would you know that he was even aware of that connection? He could have simply been a relatively devout Muslim—not even a fundamentalist—who worshiped at that mosque because it was the most convenient. Erring on the side of caution you might well write in a report, 'this individual was involved with activities at a mosque known to be connected to al-Qaeda.'

"At the same time, just as there probably was competition between anti-armor teams, to see which one scored the most 'kills' against Taliban armored vehicles, there was likely some sort of rivalry between intelligence teams. You want your team to have the best success rate. In combat in Vietnam, that meant that if you had a body in black pajamas, he was obviously Vietcong. In the context of intelligence operations in Afghanistan, say you're interrogating a guy with a turban and beard. He must be Taliban or al-Qaeda. Write it up well, he goes to Guantánamo and your team scores.

High scores of this kind, Christino said, might well benefit a soldier's career, and they would be recorded in his formal evaluation. "A sergeant with a bullet on his report that read, 'interrogated over X detainees in Afghanistan; Y were sent on to Guantánamo' would certainly look very good to a promotion board."

The last element in the picture Christino described is the failure of any check or balance. As decisions and classifications were passed up the chain of command, there would be few willing to "question the party line," or again, to take the risk of freeing a detainee whom someone else had designated as a likely terrorist. The screeners were supposed to cross-refer their information with U.S. intelligence databases. In practice, however, this analysis was usually superficial. If a detainee had been accused of training at a particular camp and the database suggested such a place had never existed, he might be lucky. Other false allegations were unlikely to be spotted. Moreover, even this basic check was not always available at Kandahar, the last stop for most Gitmo-bound detainees. Lieutenant Colonel Saul's report reveals that at Kandahar "FM and cell phone connectivity was sporadic. An effect of poor communications was that the [intelligence] teams did not have access to the source databases, nor did they have access to intelligence collected by other HUMINT agencies in the country."

On both sides of the Atlantic, the criminal law shares a doctrine. What it terms "the fruit of the poisoned tree," evidence from a tainted source, should never be admissible in court. The flaws in the Afghan screening process described by Christino and in Saul's report are so deep they call into question every Gitmo detention. But, poisoned as this tree may have been, its toxins continue to pervade every nook and cranny of Guantánamo Bay.

2

THE LEAST WORST PLACE

Prisoners of war must at all times be humanely treated. . . . Prisoners of war must at all times be protected, particularly against acts of violence or intimidation and against insults and public curiosity . . . Prisoners of war shall be quartered under conditions as favorable as those for the forces of the Detaining Power who are billeted in the same area . . . In no case shall disciplinary punishments be inhuman, brutal or dangerous to the health of prisoners of war.

—Convention (III) Relative to the Treatment of
Prisoners of War, Geneva, August 12, 1949

In the beginning—January 2002—as Camp X-ray's cells began to fill and their occupants tried to adjust to the idea of being held at a place that felt like the end of the earth, the open metal cages were its only solid structure. A few miles away, beyond a fetid, reedy swamp cut by a blacktop highway, the Guantánamo Bay naval base was an outpost of American civilization, blessed with an officers' dining club, a shopping mall, a McDonald's restaurant, residential subdivisions and an elementary school. These air-conditioned comforts were denied to Camp X-ray's inmates and guards alike. The marines assigned to be the first guards lived in tents, prey for Gitmo's myriad bugs and relentless tropical heat.

When the skies opened in the afternoon, as they often did, the ground of their encampment turned to steaming mud.

Their minds stoked by the rhetoric of America's generals and political leaders, the guards seemed to be thoroughly scared of the detainees, *The Miami Herald*'s Carol Rosenberg told me. "They'd been told they were rabid terrorists, who could rip their throats out." A few days after the camp first opened, Rosenberg and a few of her colleagues were taken to observe it from a nearby hill. As they peered through binoculars, they were astonished to see bound detainees, shackled to gurneys, being wheeled from their cages to their first interrogations. The photographers in the group worked furiously, producing another set of devastating images that were swiftly disseminated around the world. Their publication brought a swift change in policy: After that, prisoners walked, albeit shackled, to be interrogated.

The regime described by former prisoners who survived the camp's first weeks was extreme. "You weren't allowed to talk to the person in the next cell," Asif Iqbal recalled. "You couldn't turn to face Mecca at prayer time. And the food was absolutely terrible: a little pile of rice and a few beans in the middle of an enormous plate. We used to call it *nouvelle cuisine,* American style." Aside from interrogations, there was nothing to do. Guantánamo's exotic wildlife often paid visits. The Australian David Hicks became famous in Camp X-ray for his skill at capturing mice. Shafiq Rasul said, "We had these canteens, which had no lids, so we used to stuff our towels in them to stop the frogs getting in." Soaked by the afternoon rains, they also had to endure hours without protection, exposed to the burning sun.

At night, they said, they were told to sleep with their hands outside their blankets, illuminated by bright electric lights. "One night I fell asleep and my hands slipped under the blankets," Rasul said. "They started throwing rocks at my cage." Their meager "comfort items" would be removed for the least infringement of the camp's arbitrary rules—it was even forbidden, Rasul said, to lean against the cell's mesh walls. In the background always lay the threat of violence. "One guy got hold of something unauthorized—a little piece of string. The guards dragged him out and pinned him to the ground." Mohammed Saghir, a Pakistani sawmill owner in his fifties who was interviewed by James Meek of *The Guardian* after his release in 2003, said that in this period, "they wouldn't let us call for prayers or pray in the room [cell]. I tried to pray and four or five commandos came and they beat me up. If someone would try to make a call for prayer they would beat him up and gag him."

When I first published parts of the freed detainees' stories in the spring of 2004, the Pentagon denounced them as "spurious and unsubstantiated." But as time has gone on, more and more of what they said has been corroborated, especially by the disclosures made in the wake of the prisoner abuse in Iraq. Their account of Camp X-ray's beginnings is now confirmed by internal Gitmo documents. For example, Asif Iqbal and Shafiq Rasul told me that the chains in which they were flown from Afghanistan had cut them, causing them pain. In one of the documents, a Gitmo official admits that many of the prisoners had severe "skin abrasions, caused by the shackles during the flight from Afghanistan. We will send a message to Afghanistan alerting them to the problem."

On January 20, 2002, the International Committee of the Red Cross was allowed to visit Gitmo for the first time. Its three delegates, Urs Boegli, Paul Bonard and Dr. Raed Arurabi, raised many concerns, which were later reflected in an extraordinary task force memo. For example, the Red Cross had pointed out that none of the detainees knew where they were, and that in many Arab countries, red or orange jumpsuits were "a sign that someone is about to be put to death." There were, therefore, some "issues for the commander," the memo's anonymous author wrote. "Should we continue not to tell them what is going on and keep them scared? I.C.R.C. says they are very scared. What are the benefits in keeping them scared vs. telling them what is happening? . . . The detainees think they are being taken to be shot." The prisoners, the memo added, "were having a hard time sleeping when their hands have to be visible. Guards wake them." The camp commander should also "check into lowering the lights at night to help with sleeping," and decide whether the prisoners' enforced silence could be lifted. He should also consider whether it might be possible to allow "closely trimmed beards."

The Red Cross visit ended with a meeting with Camp X-ray's senior officers on January 21. At times, the meeting's minutes record, the discussion was surreal. For example, prisoners had complained bitterly about their lack of privacy when they wished to use the toilet. According to the minutes: "Guards escort shackled detainees to the toilet. At the toilet, a detainee's left hand is freed from his hand shackle. His right hand remains shackled and held by the guard. We are considering unshackling prisoners' hands altogether at the toilet. However the door to the toilet must remain open and the detainee viewed by at least one guard." The task force officers were well aware of the stress and humiliation this procedure engendered. As the minutes state: "Men of the Muslim culture [sic] are much more sensitive about their privacy than men in the Western culture."

the dormitories, guards take almost all their meals in the cavernous mess halls. During my visit, luncheon conversation there was made more difficult by giant plasma televisions, on which were being relayed speeches and press conferences by Donald Rumsfeld. There were, however, free ice-cream stations. A sign said these had been provided as a means of "recognizing our troops' contribution to the global war on terror."

Phoning home from Gitmo has to be done from open-air phones exposed to the broiling sun, and, thanks to a monopoly held by the communications firm LCN, calls to America cost up to 53 cents a minute. Cell phones do not function, and Internet links are erratic. In the summer of 2003, the arrest of Gitmo's Muslim chaplain, Captain James Yee, and two Arabic translators on suspicion of espionage made it still harder for Joint Task Force members to stay in touch with their loved ones. Laptop computers are now liable to inspection at any time and whenever their owners leave Guantánamo. "Some of us may have personal messages or photographs of our wives and spouses that we don't want the world looking at," said Captain Gregg Langevin, thirty-three, ordinarily a family man and McDonald's corporation sales manager from Worcester, Massachusetts. Describing his own communications home, Charles McPeak, drafted from a job as a wholesale florist in Michigan to patrol Camp Delta as a military policeman, said: "I just say the fishing's good, the weather's hot, and I'm working on my tan. I try to email every day. It's a tough mission."

Langevin had already been mobilized on an earlier occasion after 9/11, when he was drafted to guard the Canadian border. Like many soldiers, he had stayed in the reserves after leaving active duty eight years earlier in order to preserve his retirement pay, little imagining he might find himself assigned to a place such as Gitmo. "When I get home I've got a decision to make—whether to resign and lose my entitlement, or accept the prospect of another tour like this one." The demands of fighting the war on terror have imposed this choice on many American families. Langevin told me he kept going by resolving each morning to keep himself cheerful and by believing in his sense of mission. On the one hand, he felt safer walking through Camp Delta than past his local Massachusetts high school, albeit that in Camp Delta, there was a "lot more security." But like the guards Pearson and Morales, he had taken Rumsfeld's messages to heart: "These people have a different cultural mind-set. They would think nothing of driving a bus full of explosives into a building, and they think God's telling them to do that."

Images of 9/11 abound at Gitmo. In the hot, flyblown shack that guards use to send their emails home, a poster with a picture of the World Trade Center's twin towers asks: "Are you in a New York state of mind? Don't leak information—our enemy can use it to kill U.S. troops or more innocent people." Other icons have been left in painted concrete in the "rock garden," where departing units memorialize their tour of duty. Among the most elaborate is a waist-high model of the towers, swaddled by the Stars and Stripes. It was built by members of the 240th Military Police Company at the end of their stay in August 2003, who adorned it with this legend: "That's why we're here—to defend FREEDOM." Whenever two members of the Joint Task Force may happen to meet, they are supposed to enact a little ritual. Above Camp Delta's main gate is a banner bearing Operation Enduring Freedom's motto: "Honor Bound to Defend Freedom." As the two soldiers approach, they are supposed to salute. One will say

"Honor bound," and the second will reply, "to defend freedom."
By such means the U.S. Army tries to maintain morale.

Shortly before my visit, on the seaward side of the prison, the
camp authorities had just opened an evening bar called Club
Survivor. It is a place to watch the sun go down over a Jamaican
beer. There, several guards told me their marriages were in trouble, their kids going off the rails. One refrain I heard repeatedly
provided a bare consolation: "This may be tough, but at least it's
not Iraq."

Lonely and tedious as a guard's existence is, what I could see of
the life of a detainee was rather less tolerable. Camp Delta's
perimeter fence is covered by thick, green tarpaulins, so that inside, the one relief from Gitmo's pervading heat and dust—the
sparkling blue ocean—is invisible. Even without the tarps, however, most of the detainees—the 550 in "maximum security"
conditions—would get few opportunities to look at the view.
The best they can hope for, in return for behaving compliantly
and "cooperating" with their interrogators, is to be led in handcuffs and leg irons from their cells to a small, covered yard for
twenty minutes of exercise in the company of one other detainee, followed by a shower and change of clothes, five days a
week. Less amenable detainees will enjoy this privilege only
twice in the same period. I was shown around an empty cellblock
by a sergeant from Arkansas. "After several days, won't a prisoner
and his clothing be quite sweaty?" I asked. The sergeant
shrugged.

Kellogg Brown & Root's standard issue Gitmo cell is a pre-
fabricated metal box, painted a faded green, a little larger than a
king-size bed: fifty-six square feet. Next to the hard steel wall-

mounted bed, two-and-a-half feet wide, is an Asian-style toilet (a hole in the floor) facing the open grille of the door. The guards, some of them women, are supposed to pass by the cell every thirty seconds. Next to the toilet is a small sink and a single faucet that produces tepid water that comes from a desalination plant. Like all the water at Gitmo, it's a pale shade of yellow. The faucet is so low that the only way to use it is to kneel. According to the Pentagon, the faucets are low for a reason: "To accommodate Muslim foot-washing needs."

Cells of this size are not uncommon in maximum security American prisons, although in many states, inmates—even those on death row—may spend hours each day in less confined conditions, working or associating with other prisoners. They will also normally have unrestricted access to television, books, music and letter-writing materials, and they can receive frequent visitors.

Of course, at Gitmo, none of the detainees has been convicted of a crime, but there, at the highest security level, the occupants of such cells are not allowed to keep even a cup. If they wish to drink, they must either bend and drink from the faucet or attract the attention of a guard. They are also given the following items: a thin mattress and a blanket; one set of orange clothing, consisting of a T-shirt, boxer shorts and trousers; a toothbrush, soap and shampoo; and a prayer cap, prayer mat and copy of the Koran. There is no air conditioning in the cellblocks. When the temperature inside reaches 86 degrees Fahrenheit, the guards are permitted to switch on ceiling fans—not in the cells, but the corridor. The lights stay on all night.

Echoing Rumsfeld's promise that conditions at Gitmo are "humane," the public affairs staff lay heavy emphasis on the fact that prisoners are fed only with food deemed to be *halal* under the strict requirements of Islam, while each cot is etched with an arrow to indicate the direction of Mecca, which Muslims must face in prayer. But for those who have experienced it, indefinite detention in such conditions is a harsh punishment in and of itself. Meals—on the day I visited the kitchen, lunch was a distinctly unappetizing egg curry—must be taken alone. "Time speeds up," Shafiq Rasul said. "You just stare and the hours go clicking by. You'd look at people and see they'd lost it. There was nothing in their eyes anymore. They didn't talk." In the times when he was held with fellow English-speakers, conversations between the occupants of different cells would usually turn to food: "You'd say, 'Can you remember eating this food, that food?' And everyone would chip in with their recollections of that particular dish."

Having visited Camp Delta's kitchens, I understood the obsession. Three times a week, detainees would get scrambled eggs for lunch. Once a fortnight, detainees judged the trustiest and most cooperative would be rewarded with what the cooks called a "feast": a foam tray with a little hummus, dates and salad. Once a year, for the Muslim holiday of the Eid, they would get baklava pastry. Conversation was equally monotonous, Rasul said. "You'd ask if the others had heard a particular joke or funny story. Usually you'd get the reply, 'Yeah, five times.' " Sometimes, he said, they would be taken to see psychiatrists. The response to any complaint was always the same: an offer to administer Prozac.

It is possible that for some detainees, religion may provide some solace. The evidence suggests not all. My visit took place shortly before the Muslim holy month, Ramadan, when even the least observant believer in a Muslim country will fast daily from dawn to dusk. The camp kitchens had made special arrangements to accommodate this, said the chefs, contractors from the Pentad Corporation of Las Vegas: Meals could be taken during the hours of darkness. But 20 percent of the detainees—more than 120—had asked to be given their breakfast and lunch in the normal way. If, as their captors claimed, they entered Camp Delta as Islamic fundamentalists, then they seemed to have lost their faith.

In any event, a Muslim prisoner will not find much spiritual help from the camp authorities. When Captain James Yee, the Muslim chaplain, was arrested and cast into a military prison in September 2003, charged with mishandling classified documents, he was not replaced. (After months of solitary confinement in a brig in South Carolina, he was eventually cleared of any security breach.) The Geneva Convention states that prisoners should be able to exercise "complete latitude" in the practice of religion, and they should be able to choose religious leaders from among their number. This, however, the Joint Task Force is not prepared to permit. Yee's duties—ministering to Muslims among both the Americans and the detainees—were assumed by the task force's head chaplain, Colonel Steve Feehan.

A burly, balding figure who had served God in uniform for nineteen years, I asked Feehan about his personal faith. "I'm from the conservative strand of the Southern Baptist church." So was he a fundamentalist? "I believe the Bible is literally true. Yes, the world was created in seven days." What about those who did not share his faith in Christ? "Without believing in and accepting Christ, without faith, you cannot be redeemed. It's impossible." According to the man responsible for the detainees' spiritual welfare, they were heading for eternal damnation.

* * *

Back in the days of Camp X-ray, its hospital was housed in tents and its staff were kept busy. In Kandahar, men with bullet and shrapnel injuries had not been properly treated. At Gitmo, the doctors had to perform amputations and deal with suppurating wounds. None of the prisoners on the third flight from Kandahar could walk and, like those going to the first interrogations, were unloaded from their aircraft shackled to gurneys.

The hospital I saw was made from steel and concrete, an air-conditioned, white-walled refuge from the relentless tropical heat. Its operating room was said to be the equal of any in America; there were three spotless wards and a dental facility. But instead of the trauma wrought by combat, the Guantánamo medics were spending their time treating wounds of the psychological variety, inflicted not by shrapnel but arduous, indefinite imprisonment. In 2002, there were several cases of tuberculosis. A year later, the only epidemic was depression.

To the right of the hospital reception area was a physiotherapy unit, generously equipped with specialized machines. At the time of my visit, its only patient was a man who in January 2003 hanged himself with a sheet inside his cell. By the time the guards could cut him down he was in a coma, with irreversible brain damage. Unconscious for three-and-a-half months, he would never walk again unaided, although he did relearn to speak. "He'll need full-time care for the rest of his life," said the hospital's number two, Dr. Louis Louk, a naval surgeon-commander from Florida.

In the camp's acute ward lay a young man, chained to his bed, being fed high-protein and vitamin mush through a stomach tube inserted in one of his nostrils. At the time of my visit, he had eaten nothing for fifty days, and so he had been forcibly nourished through the tube for four-and-a-half weeks. "He's refused to eat 148 consecutive meals," Dr. Louk said with clinical precision. Then came a flash of anger. "In my opinion, he's a spoiled brat, like a small child who stomps his feet when he doesn't get his way." Why was Dr. Louk so critical of this patient? "The interpreter can't get any rhyme or reason from him as to why he won't eat. All he needs now is fattening up." Why was he shackled? "I don't want any of my guys to be assaulted or hurt," Dr. Louk said. When the force-feeding began, Dr. Louk's patient weighed 116 pounds. Had any of the medical staff been assaulted before? As far as he knew, Dr. Louk said, the answer was no.

The rate of suicide attempts by inmates—whose official total reached thirty-two by the end of September 2003—has recently declined. This, however, has only been achieved because most of the detainees' attempts to hang themselves have been reclassified. Gitmo has apparently spawned an outbreak of a very rare form of self-harm—the "manipulative self-injurious behavior," or SIB. That, said chief surgeon Captain Stephen Edmondson, meant "the individual's state of mind is such that they did not sincerely want to end their own life." Instead, Edmondson and his colleagues believe that the prisoners thought they could get better treatment or even obtain release by tying a noose around their necks. Many SIBs would previously have been recorded as would-be suicides, Edmondson admitted. "We developed the manipulative definition over time as we became more familiar with this operation." In the previous six months, there had been forty such incidents—almost two each week. (At the time of writing in June 2004, Gitmo's spokesman Lieutenant Colonel Leon Sumpter told me in an email that the attempted suicide total has crept up by just two, to thirty-four. "The last attempt dates back to January 2004," he said. "Not only has our guard force and medical staff acted quickly to prevent any incidents from occurring, but there is also a camp-wide emphasis on mental health care.")

Why did Dr. Edmondson think so many of the prisoners were depressed? Perhaps they had been mentally ill before they were captured, he suggested. Just possibly, "their detention may be a factor." But overall, "you just can't put your finger on it." What if a prisoner had received bad news from home by letter, I asked. Bearing in mind that detainees' letters, transmitted via the Red Cross and subject to military censorship, were subject to long delays, would Dr. Edmondson allow them to use a telephone? "I'm not going to give them a phone," he said, grimacing.

At an international conference in San Antonio, I tracked down Daryl Matthews, professor of Forensic Psychiatry at the University of Hawaii, who was asked by the Pentagon to spend a week at Guantánamo in 2003, investigating detainees' mental health and the psychiatric treatments the camp had available. Unlike reporters—who before they can even board their military plane for Gitmo must sign strict conditions agreeing on pain of immediate removal not to try to speak to prisoners—Professor Matthews spoke with the prisoners for many hours.

Manipulative self-injurious behavior was "not a psychiatric classification," he said, and the Pentagon should not be using it. "Suicide is not a unitary phenomenon, and there are a lot of different reasons why people attempt it. It is dangerous to try to divide 'serious' attempts at suicide from mere gestures, and a psychiatrist needs to make a proper diagnosis in each and every case, to ask why that particular individual is trying to take his life." At Gitmo, Dr. Matthews added, making such diagnoses is more difficult than usual because of the "huge cultural gulf" between the detainees and their doctors, nurses and guards. "If you don't treat suicide attempts with drugs, you have to treat them with intimacy. But the barriers to intimacy there are considerable."

Gitmo's reclassification of attempted suicide might be more convincing if it did not take place against a background of widespread mental illness, especially depression. Chief surgeon Edmondson told me that the drugs most commonly prescribed for detainees were Prozac and similar mood-enhancing pills. More than one-fifth of Camp Delta's inmates were taking them. There are thirty-five cells in Gitmo's new mental health facility, four of them equipped with restraints for prisoners bent on self-harm. "There's people in that block who were smearing their feces on their cell walls," Shafiq Rasul said. "These guys were okay when they came, and they're like that now."

The International Committee of the Red Cross was already worried about prisoners' mental health by the late summer of 2002. According to the minutes of a meeting on September 9 with Camp Delta's then-commandant, Brigadier General Rick Baccus, the Red Cross representative Daniel Cavoli was told that fifty-three detainees were receiving "mental health counseling." As his I.C.R.C. predecessors had done in January 2002, Cavoli asked Baccus to reduce detainees' stress by grouping them together by language, but Baccus refused. (At one stage, Asif Iqbal spent five months in a block where all the other prisoners were citizens of China, and he spoke no English at all.) A year after Cavoli's visit, the International Committee of the Red Cross, which is normally extremely reluctant to jeopardize its privileged access to prison camps by criticizing them in public, took the unusual step of informing the media of its concerns. "We have observed what we consider to be a worrying deterioration in the psychological health of a large number of the internees," said its spokesman, Florian Westphal. There was no mystery about the principal reason. "They have no idea about their fate and they have no means of recourse at their disposal through any legal mechanism. As [they] spend more time in Guatánamo and continue to have no idea what is going to happen to them, we are concerned that the impact on them will get more serious."

Daryl Matthews, who has long experience of working in prisons, reached a similar conclusion. In any correctional facility, the stresses on prisoners were very high: the lack of privacy or exercise; the forced proximity to other inmates and guards; boredom and the possibility of violence. But Gitmo, he said, "is prison plus. The stressors are incredible. A prisoner has at least some access to due legal process, to legal counsel, and if he or she has been convicted, an idea of how much longer they have to stay locked up. At Guantánamo, the detainees don't know whether they'll ever get out, or even why they are there. Ordinary prisoners have visits with their family, but at Camp Delta they're almost entirely sealed off from the community." He cited an additional factor: "In prison, relationships between inmates and guards are pretty affirming. Here, they come from two universes, separated by an unbelievable gulf." Matthews put all this in his official report for the Pentagon. He has not been asked to visit Gitmo again.

Camp Delta's chief of detention, in charge of security and prisoner welfare, was Sergeant Major Anthony Mendez, a career military corrections officer with twenty-six years' experience. Inadvertently he confirmed Matthews's diagnosis. In any ordinary prison, he said, staff made assiduous efforts to build relationships between inmates and guards. At Camp Delta, "we discourage that," and in order to prevent such relationships developing, the guard details assigned to each block were changed every day. If he detected any sign of a guard "getting personal" with a detainee, he would take immediate action. In America, he added, "our philosophy is some kind of rehabilitation. That's not our purpose here, that's not our mission."

In Pakistan's Swat Valley in late 2003, *The Guardian's* James Meek interviewed Shah Mohamed, then aged twenty-three, a baker, who had tried to choke himself by lashing a sheet through the mesh of his cage four times. At first, he seemed vague about the reasons, mentioning his fears for his mother's health and other troubles back home. Then it emerged that his attempts began after he was held for a month in a sealed punishment cell without explanation. There, Mohamed told Meek, "there were no windows. There were four walls and a roof made of tin, a light bulb and an air conditioner. They put the air conditioning on and it was extremely cold. They would take away the blanket in the morning and bring it back in the evening." He said he had been forcibly injected with a psychotropic drug: "I refused and they brought seven or eight people and held me and injected me. I couldn't see down, I couldn't see up . . . I couldn't think or do anything. They just told me: 'Your brain is not working properly.'" Cleared of any involvement in terrorism, Mohamed was one of the first detainees to be released.

On my tour of Camp Delta, I caught only glimpses of the detainees: shadows being moved among the lanes of razor wire, hidden by the ubiquitous tarpaulins. As Captain Langevin had told

me, "The camp seems disciplined; there's no banging and shout-
ing, like in civilian jails. It's silent. Maybe it's the heat." But as I
passed through the main gate, for a second the façade cracked.
From somewhere unseen came a hiss: "Liars! Liars! Nazi liars!" I
was with two fellow reporters and Sergeant Major Mendez.
"Does it worry you when they call you a Nazi?" I asked. Mendez
chuckled. "What, the detainees or my men?" Everything possible
had been done to create an impression of smooth, effortless effi-
ciency. But there is, I was subsequently to learn, a very different
side to Gitmo.

Inside Camp Delta, Shafiq Rasul told me, "there's only one
rule that matters. You have to obey whatever U.S. government
personnel tell you to do." The costs of disobedience, he went
on, would be high. Another internal Gitmo document, headed
"Detainee Standards of Conduct," suggests he was telling the
truth.

"The following is a set of standards Detainees **WILL** follow
at **ALL** times," it begins. "Failure to follow the following standards will result in *strict punishment* by U.S. security forces." (My
italics.) The first two rules allow thirty minutes for detainees to
eat their meals and just five minutes for showers, although here
"amputees are authorized 10–15 minutes for showers." Then the
rules become more menacing:

(3) Detainees **WILL NOT** be disrespectful to any U.S.
Security Forces personnel or other detainees.
(4) Detainees **WILL** follow the orders of U.S. Security
Forces at ALL times.
(5) Detainee units can and **WILL** be searched at any time.
(6) Detainees **WILL NOT** harass, annoy, harm or otherwise

interfere with the safety or operation of the detention facility.

(7) Detainees **WILL NOT** touch, spit or throw any object at U.S. Security Forces personnel or other detainees. If any non-issued objects are found in or around unit area, detainees **WILL** inform U.S. Security Forces, with no disciplinary action taken.

(8) Detainees **WILL** keep noise down to a low conversational level. At no time will a detainee be allowed to yell or become unruly. At **NO** time will detainees communicate across block unit areas.

(9) Detainees **WILL** at all times display their comfort items in the front of their unit in the following order:

   a. Soap
   b. Shower shoes
   c. Toothpaste
   d. Toothbrush
   e. Small towel
   f. Water bottle

The next three rules allow detainees to hang a towel across their windows to block the sun, promise fifteen minutes of exercise twice a week, and permit the Koran to be hung from the cells' wall units. It is perhaps the last rule that is the most sinister:

(13) U.S. Security Forces **RESERVE THE RIGHT** to alter or temporarily cease the above standards if necessary.

Gitmo's public affairs spokesmen will not disclose the details of the "strict punishment" threatened in the document's preamble. "We do not discuss operational aspects of the J.T.F. mission,"

Lieutenant Colonel Sumpter told me by email. We must, therefore, rely on the accounts of freed detainees, one of whose more
striking features is the extent to which they mutually corrobo-
rate. Sometimes, they have said, prisoners accused of breaching
Camp Delta discipline were placed in an isolation cell. More
often, they were attacked by Gitmo's punishment squad—the
ERF, or "Extreme Reaction Force." (Some reports have termed
this unit the "Internal Reaction Force," but the other usage appears to be more common, and it was not corrected in my email
correspondence with Sumpter.) Shafiq Rasul said these assaults
became so familiar to detainees that they coined a new verb: to be
"ERFed." One of the most vivid descriptions was given to me by
Tarek Dergoul:

"They'd already searched me and my cell twice that day,
gone through my stuff, touched my Koran, felt my body, around
my private parts," he said. "And now they wanted to do it again,
just to provoke me, but I said no, because if you submit to everything, you turn into a zombie. I heard a guard talking into his
radio, "ERF, ERF, ERF," and I knew what was coming. The five
cowards, I called them, five guys running in with riot gear. They
pepper sprayed me in the face, and I started vomiting; in all I must
have brought up five cupfuls. They pinned me down and attacked me, poking their fingers in my eyes, and forced my head
into the toilet pan and flushed. They tied me up like a beast and
then they were kneeling on me, kicking and punching. Finally
they dragged me out of the cell in chains, into the rec[reation]
yard, and shaved my beard, my hair, my eyebrows."

Dergoul said he was "ERFed" four or five times, always on
the pretext that he had committed some minor breach of the
rules. His fellow British detainees, Asif Iqbal, Ruhal Ahmed and

Shafiq Rasul, also described ERF assaults: In Rasul's experience, ERFing meant "being slammed against the floor by a soldier wielding a riot shield, pinned to the ground and beaten up by five armored men." Soon after the move from Camp X-ray to Delta, he told me, he witnessed the especially brutal beating of an inmate from Bahrain, who was palpably disturbed and used to spend most of the day and night "making strange animal noises."

In May 2004, further details were included in a letter, jointly signed by Iqbal and Ahmed, to the Senate Armed Services Committee: "[He] was lying on the floor of his cage immediately near to us when a group of eight or nine guards known as the ERF Team (Extreme Reaction Force) entered his cage. We saw them severely assault him. They stamped on his neck, kicked him in the stomach even though he had metal rods there as a result of an operation, and they picked up his head and smashed his face into the floor. One female officer was ordered to go into the cell and kick him and beat him, which she did, in his stomach." A fifth freed Briton, Jamal al-Harith, told the *Los Angeles Times* he both experienced and witnessed "dozens" of ERF beatings: "I have spoken to the people this has happened to. I have seen the effects. I have seen people beat up—the swollen faces, the limping back or being dragged back. I've seen the effects of it."

The depiction of prisoner abuse at Abu Ghraib notwithstanding, as of the end of May 2004, the Pentagon was still insisting that the claims of beatings by the former detainees were "not credible," and therefore did not require investigation. "The allegations being made by these individuals are untrue," a spokesman said. Then, in early June, news broke of Specialist Sean Baker, a former Gitmo military policeman and guard, who was discharged from the U.S. Army because of injuries he sustained while pretending to be a prisoner during an all-too-realistic ERF exercise. In January 2003, he was told to put on an orange detainee jumpsuit over his uniform and crawl under a bunk in a cell so that the ERF—who had been told he was a genuine detainee who had already assaulted a sergeant—could practice.

Baker told his local Kentucky television station: "They grabbed my arms, my legs, twisted me up and unfortunately one of the individuals got up on my back from behind and put pressure down on me while I was facedown. Then he—the same individual—reached around and began to choke me and press my head down against the steel floor. After several seconds, twenty to thirty seconds, it seemed like an eternity because I couldn't breathe, I began to panic and I gave the code word I was supposed to give to stop the exercise, which was 'red' . . . That individual slammed my head against the floor and continued to choke me. Somehow I got enough air. I muttered out: 'I'm a U.S. soldier. I'm a U.S. soldier.'"

After receiving first aid at Gitmo, Baker was evacuated to a hospital in Portsmouth, Virginia, and after a fortnight there sent home to rest. Unfortunately, he began to develop seizures and had to be admitted to the Walter Reed Army Medical Center for treatment of a traumatic brain injury, where he stayed for forty-eight days. After being transferred to light duty, he was finally discharged from the military in April 2004. Initially, Major Laurie Arellano of Southern Command in Miami told reporters that Baker's condition was unrelated to the injuries he had suffered in the ERF drill. However, the Army's Physical Evaluation Board stated the following in a document dated September 29, 2003: "The T.B.I. [traumatic brain injury] was due to soldier playing role of detainee who was non-cooperative and was being extracted from detention cell in Guantánamo Bay, Cuba, during a training exercise."

Baker told reporters and his lawyer that the entire exercise had been videotaped: Unaccountably, the tape was said to have disappeared. My own investigations have now confirmed that each and every ERF deployment is filmed, as a matter of standing routine. "There was always this guy behind the squad, filming everything that happened," Tarek Dergoul told me, and Shafiq Rasul and Jamal al-Harith made similar assertions.

When I put the claim to the Gitmo spokesman Lieutenant Colonel Sumpter, he confirmed it, saying that all ERF actions were filmed so that they could be "reviewed" by senior officers— as a way of ascertaining whether the squads were using disproportionate force. All the tapes were kept in an archive at Guantánamo, he said. He refused to say how many times the ERF squads had been used, and he would not discuss their training or rules of engagement. All these questions met the same, familiar response: "We do not discuss operational aspects of the Joint Task Force mission." In late July 2004, the Associated Press quoted a Gitmo spokesman saying that "only" 32 hours of 500 hours of tape revealed the FRF using excessive force.

At the time of writing, Senator Patrick Leahy, the ranking Democrat on the Senate Judiciary Committee, has written to Donald Rumsfeld, demanding that the ERF videos be produced. "Congressional oversight of this administration has been lax in many areas, including detention policy in Iraq, Afghanistan and Guantánamo," he said. "It is past time for that to change. If photos, videotapes or any other evidence exists that can help establish whether or not there has been mistreatment of prisoners at Guantánamo Bay, it should be provided without delay to the Congress."

"After what's happened at Abu Ghraib, if I'd been the Americans, I would have destroyed those videos," Tarek Dergoul told me. "Let them be shown. Then the world will know I'm telling the truth." Shortly before his release in March 2004, Dergoul said, a new punishment had been introduced: transfer to "Romeo block," where prisoners would be held in isolation, usually half-naked, for days at a time. A fuller description was included in the letter to the Senate from Iqbal, Rasul and Ahmed: "[In] what was called the Romeo block . . . they would be stripped completely. After three days they would be given underwear. After another three days they would be given a top, and then after another three days given trouser bottoms. Some people only ever got underwear. This was said to be for 'misbehaving.' " What might count as "misbehaving"? It might, Rasul said, be something as trivial as having two cups inside one's cell, instead of the permitted one.

Needless to say, no prisoner was ever given any kind of hearing for any alleged disciplinary breach, as would be mandatory in an ordinary penitentiary. As the Gitmo rules state: "Failure to follow the following standards *will* result in strict punishment" (my italics).

Behind Gitmo's Potemkin façade, it seems close to being a perfect example of what the sociologist Erving Goffman called a "total institution," in which every aspect of inmates' lives is controlled. The long-term consequences of confinement in such a place will be immense, Goffman found, and the reintegration into society of a former resident difficult or impossible. And in the case of Guantánamo, it now seems evident, the default sanction used to uphold its Draconian but ever-flexible rules is physical violence.

Just how this, as Bush and Rumsfeld assert, conforms to the "spirit" or "principles" expressed by Geneva Convention III is difficult to see. The standards and rules of confinement at Guantánamo do not breach the convention only in minor, technical ways, but in its absolute fundamentals: If one sought to construct and manage a prison camp with Geneva as a blueprint, it would not resemble Camp Delta in any significant way. Detainees would, for example, be able to move freely within a secure perimeter and, instead of being subject to the all-encompassing rigor of a total institution, they would largely organize their own lives. According to the convention's Article 21: "The Detaining Power may subject prisoners of war to internment. It may impose on them the obligation of not leaving, beyond certain limits, the camp where they are interned, or if the said camp is fenced in, of not going outside its perimeter." They may not be placed in cells or cages—what the convention calls "close confinement"—other than "to safeguard their health and then only during the continuation of the circumstances which make such confinement necessary."

Under Geneva's Article 38, "The Detaining Power shall encourage the practice of intellectual, educational, and recreational pursuits, sports and games amongst prisoners, and shall take the measures necessary to ensure the exercise thereof by providing them with adequate premises and necessary equipment. Prisoners shall have opportunities for taking physical exercise, including sports and games, and for being out of doors. Sufficient open spaces shall be provided for this purpose in all camps." Self-evidently, the fifteen minutes of exercise in a small covered yard that is allotted Gitmo detainees twice a week does meet that requirement. As for educational and recreational pursuits, though, there are none.

There are many other differences between Guantánamo and the life of a camp as envisaged by the convention. For example, instead of being restricted to a tiny number of approved "comfort items," prisoners should be able to keep all their personal effects, except, understandably, their weapons. They should be able to elect representatives to act as intermediaries with the detaining power and to prepare their own food, and they should be housed according to language group. But perhaps the biggest departures of all from the Geneva Convention's "spirit" concern discipline and punishment. Under Geneva's Article 96, "Before any disciplinary award is pronounced, the accused shall be given precise information regarding the offences of which he is accused, and given an opportunity of explaining his conduct and of defending himself. He shall be permitted, in particular, to call witnesses and to have recourse, if necessary, to the services of a qualified interpreter. The decision shall be announced to the accused prisoner of war and to the prisoners' representative." The convention does not permit confinement in a cell for longer than thirty days. But even then, "Prisoners of war awarded disciplinary punishment shall be allowed to exercise and to stay in the open air at least two hours daily"—in other words, eight times as long as even the most favored Camp Delta inmate. Such is a flavor of the protections dismissed by the White House Chief Counsel Alberto Gonzalez as "quaint."

It is, perhaps, remarkable that some detainees at Guantánamo have, from time to time, found the strength and the will to resist. The most determined effort came in the spring of 2002 when almost the entire camp went on hunger strike. According to an official who has read the official Pentagon summary of what happened, "It began after a guard forcefully removed a towel that one of the detainees had wrapped about his head, prior to beginning Friday prayers. Word of this incident spread immediately through the camp, and detainees began to throw all health and comfort items out of their cells and refused to eat and/or participate in any interrogation." The strike persisted for more than a fortnight, the official said, and was eventually resolved with the help of the Red Cross. One of its results was the appointment of the hapless Muslim chaplain Yee, not only to minister to the detainees, but to teach a basic understanding of Islam's precepts to the guards. "For a time," said the official, "they thought they were really losing control." By the fall of that year, Yee was giving PowerPoint presentations—on issues such as the need to respect copies of the Koran—to every group of new guards.

Tarek Dergoul joined and helped to lead several less widespread strikes, and he infuriated the guards by translating their conversations from English into Arabic for the benefit of non-English speaking detainees. Some, he said, were hunger strikes and others noncooperation drives, in which detainees would refuse to attend interrogations or go to their exercise periods and showers. Naturally, this put them in peril of being ERFed. "We'd elect a block leader," he said, "and shout across the hallways in Arabic. There'd be a discussion, the action and a time would be agreed, and then the strike would take place." He paid a heavy personal price for his defiance. For more than a year, he said, he was held in isolation.

When I interviewed Dergoul in May 2004, two months after his release, the effects of his ordeal were palpable. It had taken him this long even to begin to talk about his experience, he said, and he suffered nightmares and flashbacks. After a thorough assessment, he had been accepted for a course of treatment at the Medical Foundation for the Care of Victims of Torture in London, the world's leading center for dealing with this type of post-traumatic stress. His first session was due the day after we met. "I get migraines, I'm depressed, and I suffer from memory loss," he said. "There's stuff that happened embedded in my head that I can't remember."

So much for Gitmo's regime, the passive background environment against which Camp Delta's main business, prisoner interrogation, takes place. It is time to join the frontline in the war against terror.

3

ENORMOUSLY VALUABLE INTELLIGENCE

Although the use of torture was theoretically forbidden in English witch-trials, there were many seventeenth century cases in which victims were kept awake for days, starved, beaten or otherwise ill-treated . . . As a contemporary observed, "witches, long tortured with watching and fasting, and pinched when but ready to nod, are contented causelessly to accuse themselves, to be eased of present pain."

—Sir Keith Thomas, *Religion and
the Decline of Magic*

Years of experience had enabled the N.K.V.D. to develop a technique of protracted interrogation which practically no one was able to resist . . . I had now found out why those involved in "show" trials so readily admitted every accusation, and the comparison with the medieval witch-trials no longer seemed to me to be so amusing. There are circumstances in which a human being will confess to anything.

—F. Beck and W. Godin, *Russian Purge
and the Extraction of a Confession*

Opposite Camp Delta's main gate there's a little wooden pergola, an observation point where journalists are allowed to take photographs and watch who comes and goes. Spotting the interrogators isn't difficult. Instead of battledress and sweaty black boots, they wear polo shirts, lightweight shoes, khakis or even shorts, and most of them look surprisingly young—well under thirty. Most are accompanied by older men, many of swarthy appearance—their interpreters, or, as intelligence men call them, "terps." Interrogations take place day and night, in rows of so-called "booths," bare, air-conditioned rooms inside converted trailers behind the cellblocks. Gitmo's architects and advocates say their success rate has been astounding.

Harvesting intelligence through prisoner interrogations has become Guantánamo's principal raison d'être. As of June 2004, two-and-a-half years after the camp opened, no one has been tried by the promised military commissions, and only three prisoners of the present 600 have been charged. (None of these three have been accused of specific acts of terrorism, but only of joining al-Qaeda's general conspiracy in supportive or propagandizing roles. The most serious allegations, made against the Yemeni Ali Hamza al Bahlul, are that he helped make recruitment videos.) If the political rhetoric of the early weeks first spawned the idea of a direct link between the detainees and 9/11, interrogations and their vaunted worth have maintained it, and thus enabled Gitmo's guards to cling to a sense of purpose, a way of believing that their loneliness and privations are at least doing some good. Captain Langevin from Massachusetts missed his family and was ready to resign from the reserves, even at the cost of his pension. But he kept himself going from day to day by convincing himself of the worth of his mission: "Above all else, I know that good intelligence is being gathered."

Since the days of Camp X-ray Donald Rumsfeld has emphasized this message. To be sure, he told the Miami Chamber of

Commerce in February 2004, it was time that if Guantánamo's prisoners were to be turned loose, "they would return to the fight and continue to kill innocent men, women and children." But in the meantime, "detaining enemy combatants also serves another purpose. It provides us with intelligence that can help us prevent future acts of terrorism. It can save lives and indeed I am convinced it can speed victory." Gitmo's interrogators had revealed "al-Qaeda leadership structure, operatives, funding mechanisms, communication methods, training and selection programs, travel patterns, support infrastructures and plans for attacking the United States and other friendly countries," he went on. "They've provided information on al-Qaeda front companies and on bank accounts, on surface to air missiles, improvised explosive devices and tactics that are used by terrorist elements."

During my own trip to Gitmo in October 2003, there was no more enthusiastic exponent of this mission than the Joint Task Force commandant, Major General Geoffrey D. Miller. Before we met, I had come to appreciate that he had a reputation as a strict disciplinarian: One sergeant complained that he had been bawled out for displaying his name on his army cap, which in Miller's view was unacceptable. A slight but pugnacious man, he stood in the early evening sun on the palmy bluff outside his headquarters, built on a spit that juts out into the middle of Guantánamo Bay. Our interview had began inside his office, but we had moved to the bluff to allow him to be photographed: A man of action throughout his career, General Miller explained that he did not like to be depicted behind a desk. Though short in stature, his favorite words were "enormous" and "enormously." "We are developing information of enormous value to the nation, enormously valuable intelligence," he said with evident passion. "We have an enormously thorough process that has very high resolution and clarity. We think we're fighting not only to save and protect our families, but your families also. I think of Guantánamo as the interrogation battle lab in the war against terror."

Miller had managed to impress the Pentagon with his self-assured, can-do approach. Unbeknown to me at the time of my visit, he was newly returned from Iraq, where he and a team from Guantánamo, by Donald Rumsfeld's request, had been reviewing intelligence operations at the main terrorist detention facility there—the prison near Baghdad formerly managed by Saddam Hussein, Abu Ghraib. According to Major General Janis Karpinski, who was running Abu Ghraib at the time, he was sent to "Gitmo-ize" it; in the dryer language of Major General Antonio Taguba's report on prisoner abuse there, Miller's mission in the summer of 2003 was "to review current Iraqi theater ability to rapidly exploit internees for actionable intelligence." In other words: To make them talk. As of June 2004, Miller is at Abu Ghraib once again, having been reassigned from Gitmo to take charge of military prisons throughout Iraq, despite the occupying coalition's handover to a transitional Iraqi government.

Even as the waves of the scandal triggered by the publication of photographs of abused and naked detainees at Abu Ghraib lapped around his feet, Miller retained his enormous confidence. "We're enormously proud of what we have done at Guantánamo to be able to set that kind of environment where we were focused on getting the maximum amount of intelligence," Miller said in Baghdad in May 2004, discussing his mission the previous summer. "We were bringing expertise into the theater. We made a number of recommendations, the vast majority of which were implemented following the visit."

For Geoffrey Miller, this sudden emergence as an intelligence and interrogation specialist, serving successively as leader of two of the most sensitive intelligence operations in the entire war against terror, was something of a departure. Until he went to Gitmo, he had never filled an intelligence post in his life. His specialty, from the time he attended the Field Artillery Officer Basic Course at Fort Sill, Oklahoma, in 1974 until the point in 1996 when he assumed command of the XVIII Airborne Corps Artillery at Fort Bragg, North Carolina, was in supervising the firing of big guns. (His last job before Gitmo was as assistant chief of staff in Korea.) According to Lieutenant Colonel Tony Christino, the recently retired counterterrorism intelligence specialist who was quoted extensively in chapter one of this book, "Nothing in Major General Miller's official biography suggests that he has even the least bit of expertise in intelligence. In addition to extensive service within the field artillery branch, he served in higher level operations, plans and personnel assignments. He does not appear to be well qualified either to direct strategic interrogation efforts or to assess the value of intelligence derived from such efforts." Milton Bearden, former CIA chief in Sudan and Afghanistan and later head of the agency's Soviet and Eastern Europe Division, concurred with Christino's assessment. Miller's inexperience, he said, cast doubt on the value of his mission. "You have to ask: Who appointed him? Who chose him for such a post?"

Nevertheless, from the moment Miller was assigned to Guantánamo in November 2002, increasing the camp's intelligence yield became his highest priority. His predecessor, Brigadier General Rick Baccus, was accused on departure by Pentagon officials of "coddling" the detainees; certainly the evidence from the minutes of his meetings with the Red Cross suggests that he took their welfare seriously. (It was Baccus, for example, who ordered Camp Delta's first books.) Under Baccus's command, the intelligence from Guantánamo was no more than a trickle. Of course, there are two possible reasons for this: either the prisoners may have known very little about terrorism and al-Qaeda, or they were not being questioned with sufficient skill. But Baccus did his best to prevent abuse, such as telling the task force's interrogators not to scream at detainees. "We had instances of individuals that used verbal abuse, and any time that that was reported we took action immediately and removed the individual from contact with detainees," he told *The Guardian*. "In no way did I ever interfere in interrogations, but also at that time the interrogations never forced anyone to be treated inhumanely, certainly not when I was there."

By the time of my visit in October 2003, General Miller had been in post for almost a year. He set his jaw toward the sunset as the photographer from the *Detroit Free Press* shot numerous portraits. The low, tropical light seemed to make Miller literally glow with pride. For him, intelligence was a matter of volume, of productivity, much like artillery: shells on target; statements made. "Since the beginning of July 2003, the amount of intelligence extracted from detainees each month has increased by 600 percent," Miller said. Nor did this consist of mere tidbits. "We're talking about high-value intelligence, distributed around the world."

The key to this achievement, Miller said, was a graduated system of incentives and rewards that he introduced in early 2003. The detainee who cooperated with his interrogators would be given an accumulating number of up to twenty-nine extra "comfort items," from "something as small as an added water cup, to an increased number of letters from home and books to keep in his cell, to added exercise periods and showers, up to a maximum of seven each week." As a result, 82 percent of Camp Delta's prisoners were now at the highest "privilege level," and 140 had been transferred from the claustrophobic cages to the relative ease of "Camp Four." This was a large, open compound where detainees were allowed to wear white robes instead of orange jumpsuits, to sleep ten to a communal dorm, to take their meals together on shady verandas, to shower whenever they felt dirty and, should the mood take them, play soccer or volleyball. (As I toured Camp Four, instead of the hissed hatred and whispered taunt "Nazi liars" that I had heard on leaving Camp Delta, detainees smiled and tried to engage in conversation: "Hello! What country you from?" As the Red Cross has suggested in its own reports, it is probably the only part of Gitmo that truly does come close to conformity with the "spirit" of the Geneva Convention.) Once they reached Camp Four, said Miller, detainees might well be on the way home: It was Gitmo's "decompression process."

Sometimes, he averred, interrogators might have to become "aggressive" with a noncooperative subject. But his innovations were all about the judicious use of carrots; about exploiting the incentives "to establish a rapport." Miller even suggested that Gitmo's interrogators had convinced some of their charges to talk as a way of turning their backs on their former allegiances and beliefs: "Many of the detainees have realized that the acts they did were wrong, and so they have given us information that helps us win the global war on terror." He said they had talked because they had come to admire the American values that the camp itself embodied: "I know of no country in the world which treats its enemies like the U.S. does." Miller said he had been to places such as Kuwait, Saudi Arabia and Iraq. With that experience in his mind, "I am enormously proud of what we do."

But General Miller was telling only part of the story. Behind the carrot lurked a menacing and painful stick.

Shafiq Rasul's first interrogation on reaching Gitmo came on January 16, 2002, two days after he arrived. Shackled in his "three-piece suit," he was frog-marched into a large tent where both British and American officials were waiting. "I walked in and this guy says, 'I'm from the Foreign Office. I've come from the British Embassy in America, and here is one of my colleagues who's from the Embassy as well.'" In fact, as he later learned, one of the Britons was a member of the Security Service, MI5. Rasul got to ask the first question: "Where am I?" The MI5 man replied: "We can't disclose that information." The British agent asked how he was feeling. "I started crying, saying I can't believe I'm here. He says: 'I don't want to know how you are emotionally, I'm only interested in your physical state.'"

According to the freed detainees, for most of 2002, while Brigadier General Baccus remained in charge, interrogations remained both relatively infrequent and low-key. Rasul's second session did not come for more than a month, on February 25. This time, it took place inside a wooden "sea hut," and for the first time, still wearing his three-piece suit, he was chained to a steel ring fixed into the floor. Once again there were both Americans and an MI5 man present. "They were trying to make out like I was some kind of big-timer, claiming I'd met Osama bin Laden, Mullah Omar, and I'm like, 'Where did they get that from?' " The MI5 officer showed him photographs of someone he'd never seen, he said, and told him that this individual had told his colleagues back in England that Rasul had given lectures on the need to wage jihad at the University of Wolverhampton—a place he had never visited. "The guy says to me, 'Just say you went to Afghanistan to wage jihad, that you went to fight for the Taliban, and you'll be on the way home.' I said, 'If you want me to lie just to go home, then I'll be screwing myself.' He told me he'd be at the camp for the next four days, and if I changed my mind and wanted to talk to him, he'd come back."

Altogether, the freed British detainees thought they had been interrogated five times during 2002, with no sessions at all during the second half of the year. In January 2003, as General Miller and his newly focused mission began to get into stride, there was a distinct change. The frequency and length of interrogations increased beyond recognition: In the following fifteen months, Asif Iqbal and Shafiq Rasul estimated that they were questioned almost 200 times. Meanwhile, the methods the interrogators were prepared to use had been transformed.

The Gitmo Joint Task Force is divided into two main branches: the "Joint Detention Group," responsible for every aspect of keeping the prisoners incarcerated, and the "Joint Interrogation Group," the translators, analysts and interrogators who are supposed to generate the intelligence. Geoffrey Miller's moment of insight came when he decided to merge the two functions—to use the guards, as his euphemistic phrase put it, to "set the conditions" for interrogations; or to put it another way, to soften the prisoners up. (In the little souvenir shop in the naval base mall, the detention group's acronym—JDOG—has given rise to a range of baseball caps and clothing in which it is depicted as a ferocious mastiff. On one T-shirt, the teeth of this beast are clamped firmly around a caricatured detainee's ankle.)

A Pentagon source described to me the PowerPoint presentation Miller had prepared for guards. Each incoming guard shift was to "coordinate prisoner treatment" with the intelligence teams, on the understanding that both favorable treatment and "disciplinary measures" could, in different circumstances, serve as a valuable prelude to interrogation. "It stressed that close cooperation between guards and interrogators is the surest way to achieve greater intelligence findings," the source said.

Lieutenant Commander Charles Swift, a frequent visitor to Gitmo as one of the military defense attorneys assigned to act in the planned tribunals there, supplied more details of what that meant: "The interrogators were now to be in effective control of the camp, and they have the final word. You can be a model prisoner, your behavior can be impeccable, but if you're not cooperating with the interrogators, you're going to be treated like the very worst inmate—the guy who ends up in a stripped-down cell for spitting at the guards or throwing excrement. The interrogators decide whether you're the first to eat or the last, and whether your laundry gets done, and who watches you in the shower. Or they might ask for a cell search and confiscate everything. Then it'll be the interrogator who brings it all back."

In January 2004, Major General Antonio Taguba's report on his investigation into prisoner abuse at Abu Ghraib shed further light on Miller's approach. After visiting the Baghdad jail in the summer of 2003, Miller had "concluded that Joint Strategic Interrogation Operations [within Abu Ghraib] are hampered by lack of active control of the internees within the detention environment," Taguba wrote. Miller had demanded a "unified strategy," in order to "dedicate and train a detention guard force subordinate to the Joint Interrogation Debriefing Center (JIDC) that sets the conditions for the successful interrogation and exploitation of internees/detainees . . . it is essential that the guard force be actively engaged in setting the conditions for successful exploitation of the internees." According to Taguba, "Miller's team also observed that the application of emerging strategic interrogation strategies and techniques contain new approaches and operational art."

Taguba related what the consequences were in Iraq: beatings of prisoners and sexual abuse. Sergeant Javal Davies told Taguba that interrogators had requested this of him: "Loosen this guy up for us. Make sure he has a bad night. Make sure he gets the treatment." The interrogators had thanked him and his colleague, Corporal Charles Graner, afterward, saying: "Good job, they're breaking down real fast. They answer every question. They're giving out good information." It was Graner who had forced prisoners to strip naked and simulate sex with each other, sometimes arranged in grotesque piles. Taguba asked Specialist Sabrina Harman how it was that a detainee came to be photographed while placed on a box with wires attached to his fingers, toes and penis. She stated that "her job was to keep detainees awake. M[il-itary] I[ntelligence] was talking to Corporal Graner. MI wanted to get them to talk. It is Graner's job to do things for MI . . . to get these people to talk."

At the time of writing in July 2004, there is as yet no evidence that the brutally sexualized abuse that stained America's reputation at Abu Ghraib also took place at Guantánamo. Nevertheless, the system instituted there on Miller's watch was also harshly coercive. Indeed, one reason why allegations of the undisciplined violence seen at Abu Ghraib have not surfaced at Gitmo may be that in Cuba, interrogators and guards have had more official latitude. On May 11, 2004, CENTCOM's deputy commander, General Lance Smith, told the Senate Armed Services Committee that some of the interrogation techniques authorized for use in Gitmo were banned in Iraq because there, in contrast to Cuba, prisoners were supposedly protected by the Geneva Convention. What is clear is that at every location in the global war on terror, from Washington, D.C., to Afghanistan, previous restraints on the treatment of prisoners were being reconsidered, and in significant ways abandoned. As the then–deputy assistant Attorney General John Yoo put it in a paper to the Pentagon's general counsel William J. Haynes just before Camp X-ray opened on January 9, 2002, "Restricting the President's plenary power over military operations (including the treatment of prisoners) would be constitutionally dubious."

In the intellectual and political climate created by September 11, the background assumption was that any preexisting code of conduct could be abandoned if America's aims in the war on terror so required. The key text is a memorandum by a working group led by Jay S. Bybee, then assistant Attorney General (now a federal judge) in John Ashcroft's Justice Department, dated August 1, 2002. When this was leaked almost two years later—and its frank readiness to countenance torture revealed—the White House claimed the document was "irrelevant," saying it would now be "rewritten." Subsequently, it has emerged that lawyers from all branches of the military and the intelligence agencies had participated in Bybee's group. The administration may later have had second thoughts, but at the time the memo was composed, it represented something close to a definitive picture of

American official thinking. Large parts of its text and analysis were to be reproduced verbatim in subsequent memos drawn up at the Pentagon.

Bybee's memorandum sought to establish an extremely narrow view of what torture meant. If the pain inflicted were physical, it "must rise to the level of death, organ failure, or the permanent impairment of a significant bodily function." If it were mental, "it must result in significant psychological harm of significant duration, e.g., lasting for months or even years." According to the memo, both America's domestic law against torture, a Congressional Act of 1994, and the United Nations Convention Against Torture to which the United States was a signatory "prohibit only the most extreme forms of physical or mental harm." Anything less would be merely "cruel, inhuman or degrading treatment." While this too was banned by the Convention, those responsible for such treatment would not be liable to criminal penalties.

Bybee and his colleagues based this definition—which was reproduced in many subsequent documents—on the fact that both the American statute and the U.N. convention described torture as the infliction of "severe" pain, but did not specify what "severe" meant. They went on to adopt a curious reading of the definition in Webster's dictionary, which lists the meanings of "severe" pain as "hard to endure; sharp; afflictive; distressing; violent; extreme." They were clearly being highly selective, for pain might well be sharp, afflictive and hard to endure without rising to the level of organ failure or death—indeed, there would be little point in administering any coercive technique if it were *easy* to endure. Bybee's team therefore tried to buttress their definition from a bizarre source: U.S. laws governing the payment of health insurance benefits. These laws, the memo stated, "treat severe pain as an indicator of ailments that are likely to result in permanent and serious physical damage in the absence of immediate medical treatment." If insurance companies had to pay out in cases where patients were at risk of organ failure or death, their logic ran, then to count as torture the methods used by interrogators "must rise to a similarly high level."

This definition ran counter to the long tradition of humanitarian opposition to torture and human rights jurisprudence. The whole point of the U.N. convention, said Vaughan Lowe, Chichele professor of international law at Oxford University, is that decisions as to what constitutes torture need to be decided on a case-by-case basis. "What the U.S. was trying to do here was impose its own interpretation of an international treaty unilaterally," he told me. "This is neither authoritative nor acceptable. It isn't a considered judgment or opinion, but an argument stating a very controversial point of view." At the same time, the Bybee memo "decontextualized" torture, Lowe said. The application of several techniques that individually might not be considered as torture—sleep deprivation, isolation and shackling in uncomfortable positions, for example—might easily be said to reach the level of torture when used together. Moreover, cultural factors might make a method much harder for Muslims to endure, such as the sexual abuse and deprivation of clothing used at Abu Ghraib. Overall, he commented, the memo's reasoning was of the standard he might expect from a below-average student.

For almost 400 years, torture's opponents have recognized that attempts to impose an objective definition are odious. Friedrich Spee von Langenfeld, a brave Jesuit academic from Trier, expressed this insight in his polemic against the use of torture in witch-hunts, the *Cautio Criminalis,* published in 1631. The point at which different individuals will break will vary, he wrote: The end of endurance to pressure and pain is a subjective, not an objective, phenomenon. Eventually, however, all would succumb: "It is incredible what people say under the compulsion of torture, and how many lies they will tell about themselves and about others; in the end whatever the torturers want to be true, is true." If he were an inquisitor, Spee wrote, he could exact confessions from priests and bishops. He had met an inquisitor who boasted that he could wring a confession to devil-worship out of the Pope himself.

Bybee's overrestrictive and exclusionary definition of torture was directly anticipated by this long-dead Jesuit of Trier. Writing in the midst of a terrible wave of witch-hunting zeal, when thousands of innocents were maimed under interrogation then burned at the stake, Spee noted that some techniques had been recategorized as mere "first-degree" torture, which legally did not count as torture at all. Some of these were horrible: in one such first-degree method, a suspect's shinbones were placed in iron clamps, which squeezed the flesh "like cake," until the blood was spurting from both sides. Legally, however, a witch subjected to this treatment could be said at her trial to have confessed freely, without torture.

Of course, Bybee did not advocate the return of such techniques. At the same time, his memo went on, it would be improper to rule *any* method out, because any attempt to apply the law in a way that would interfere with the President's right to determine the conduct of a war would be unconstitutional: "As Commander-in-Chief, the President has the constitutional authority to order interrogations of enemy combatants to gain intelligence information about the plans of the enemy." These powers were "especially pronounced in the middle of a war in which the nation has already suffered a direct attack . . . it may be that only successful interrogations can provide the information necessary to prevent the success of covert terrorist attacks on the United States and its citizens. Congress can no more interfere with the President's conduct of interrogations of enemy combatants than it can dictate strategy or tactical decisions on the battlefield." Moreover, if an interrogator were later to be accused of torture, he would have two lines of defense: that it was "necessary" to prevent a terrorist attack, or that it had been performed in self-defense.

Embarrassed as the administration may later have become about the memo, it would be disingenuous to underestimate its effects. Milton Bearden, former CIA officer and veteran of the secret portion of the war in Vietnam, told me this: "It doesn't matter what distribution that memo had or how tightly it was controlled. That kind of thinking will permeate the system by word of mouth. Anyone who suggests that this and other official memos on this subject didn't have an impact, doesn't know how these things work on the ground." Bearden noted that it appeared to grant immunity to those who followed the President's orders. "The message is this is coming from the top, and whatever you're doing is okay if you're doing it for the commander in chief."

Against this background, from October 2002 until April 2003, the Pentagon and its lawyers developed a menu of coercive techniques for Guantánamo in response to requests for guidance as to what might be permissible. "We'd been at this for a year-plus and got nothing out of them," one official told *The Wall Street Journal*. "We need[ed] to have a less-cramped view of what torture is and is not." Before the official menu was developed, "people were trying like hell to ratchet up the pressure," and had used methods including placing women's underwear on prisoners' heads. On October 11, 2002, the interrogators' frustration at their lack of success was set down in a memo passed up the chain of command from Gitmo's Lieutenant Colonel Jerald Phifer. "PROBLEM:" he wrote. "The current guidelines for interrogation procedures at GTMO limit the ability of interrogators to counter advanced resistance."

Their difficulties stemmed from the standard rulebook for American military interrogators, a document known as Field Manual 34–52, which begins with a clear prohibition against the use of coercive techniques: "The use of force, mental torture, threats, insults, or exposure to unpleasant and inhumane treatment of any kind is prohibited by law and is neither authorized nor condoned by the U.S. Government." Not only is this unnecessary, the manual states, it is ineffective: "The use of force is a poor technique, as it yields unreliable results, may damage subsequent collection efforts, and can induce the source to say whatever he thinks the interrogator wants to hear." Certain psychological techniques, it goes on, are permissible. They include the use of deception methods, such as what the manual calls "we know all," which might mean convincing a suspect that an associate had made a full confession that incriminated him; turning up with a fat file that was mostly blank paper; and the "good cop, bad cop" routine familiar from police procedural movies—for some reason, the manual terms this "Mutt and Jeff." The manual also allows emotional manipulation, under rubrics such as "fear up mild" and "fear up harsh" (meaning "significantly increasing the level of fear in a detainee"), "pride and ego down" (defined as "attacking or insulting the ego of a detainee"), and "emotional hate" ("playing on the hatred a detainee has for an individual or group").

At Gitmo, wrote Phifer, not even fear up harsh was enough to break resistance. He sought authorization for a range of "category two" techniques, including prolonged solitary confinement, to be given in successive doses of thirty days at a time; the use of painful "stress positions," in which prisoners would be forced to stand or sit chained doubled up for hours; continuous interrogations for periods of up to twenty hours; the removal of clothing; and "forced grooming (shaving of facial hair, etc.)." He also asked for permission to "use detainees' individual phobias (such as fear of dogs) to induce stress."

All these techniques, it is evident, would have amounted to a flagrant breach of Geneva Convention III, had Gitmo's prisoners been subject to its protection. Article 17 states: "No physical or mental torture, nor any other form of coercion, may be inflicted on prisoners of war to secure from them information of any kind whatever. Prisoners of war who refuse to answer may not be threatened, insulted, or exposed to unpleasant or disadvantageous treatment of any kind." But as America advanced down the slippery slope opened up by Bush's February 2002 order that Geneva did not apply—that even its "spirit" could be disregarded through "military necessity"—the Convention was not discussed. Nor was the fact that some of these practices, such as the use of "stress positions," have been condemned by successive U.S. governments, in the annual State Department country human rights reports. Since 2001, the State Department has denounced Burma, Egypt, Iran, Eritrea, Jordan, Libya, Saudi Arabia, Pakistan, Tunisia, Turkey and Saddam Hussein's Iraq for questioning prisoners after inflicting the pain of holding them in such stress posi-

tions. The method was routinely employed on Palestinian suspects by Israel's General Security Service, the Shin Bet, until
1999, when it was outlawed by the country's supreme court.

However, even category two methods would not always be
sufficient at Gitmo, Phifer wrote. He also sought permission for
still tougher "category three" techniques, which were "required
for a very small percentage of the most uncooperative detainees"
and "may be utilized in a carefully coordinated manner to help
interrogate exceptionally resistant detainees." They included
convincing a detainee that "death or severely painful consequences are imminent for him and/or his family," exposure to
both water and extreme cold, and, most horrifying of all, "use of
a wet towel and dripping water to induce the misperception of
suffocation." The CIA calls this technique "water-boarding," and
has reportedly deployed it against "high value" terrorist prisoners
in places other than Guantánamo. In China, Pinochet's Chile,
Robert Mugabe's Zimbawe and elsewhere it has more usually
been termed "the submarine." An Inter-American Commission
on Human Rights report in 1980 described its purpose when
used by agents of the junta in Argentina: "Immersion by means
of the so-called submarine, where the victim's head is covered
with a cloth hood and intermittently forced into a vessel contain-
ing water, [is done] in order to induce asphyxiation as a means of
obtaining information from the prisoner."

Donald Rumsfeld issued his response to Phifer's request on
November 27. Having discussed it with his deputy, Paul Wolfowitz, Undersecretary Douglas Feith and General Richard
Myers, chairman of the joint chiefs of staff, he was prepared to
authorize all the "category two" techniques, including forcible
shaving, dogs, the replacement of hot meals with cold military ra-

tions, the removal of all comfort items (even copies of the Koran), and stress positions. "I stand for 8–10 hours," Rumsfeld scrawled at the bottom of his order. "Why is standing limited to four hours?" For the time being, however, he would not permit the "submarine." The only category three method he would allow would be "use of mild non-injurious physical contact," such as "grabbing, poking in the chest, and pushing."

Six weeks later, Rumsfeld unexpectedly rescinded this order and set up another legal "working group" to reconsider what techniques were appropriate. Chaired by the Defense Department's general counsel and comprising representatives of the armed services, the Joint Chiefs of Staff and the CIA, this produced at least two long memoranda. The first, dated March 6, 2003, drew heavily on the earlier Bybee document and echoed both its definition of torture and the claim that the President had a free hand in wartime. It suggested that torture could be justified as a form of self-defense: "The nation's right to self-defense has been triggered by the events of September 11. If a government defendant were to harm an enemy combatant during an interrogation in a manner that might arguably violate criminal prohibition, he would be doing so in order to prevent further terrorist attacks on the United States by the al-Qaeda network. . . . He could argue that the executive branch's constitutional authority to protect the nation from attack justified his actions."

The memo's authors were well aware of the dark territory into which their arguments led: the war criminal's claim that he was "only following orders," and thus could not be held accountable. They even quoted the charter of the Nuremburg Nazi war crimes tribunal: "The fact that the defendant acted pursuant to the order of his government or of a superior shall not free him from responsibility." But an interrogator accused of torture could argue that his orders "may be inferred to be lawful," they suggested, and would have been "disobeyed at the peril of the subordinate." In other words, an interrogator ordered to inflict torture could justify his actions by saying he was frightened of the consequences of disobedience.

Alien detainees at Gitmo, the memo emphasized, fell outside the jurisdiction of the federal courts, and so could not claim protection from the Constitution's ban on cruel and unusual punishment. Even were their legal position to change, interrogation methods would have to "shock the conscience" to be ruled unlawful—a requirement that al-Qaeda suspects might find hard to meet in an American federal court.

The group's last memorandum on interrogation methods at Guantánamo emerged six weeks later. It took a pragmatic approach, arguing that the "choice of interrogation techniques involves a risk benefit analysis in each case." When assessing whether "exceptional" methods were appropriate, "consideration should be given to the possible adverse effects on U.S. armed forces culture and self-image, which at times past may have suffered due to perceived law of war violations." There was also a risk that extracting a confession by harsher means "may produce a statement that might be argued to be involuntary for purposes of criminal proceedings . . . the more coercive the method, the greater the likelihood that the method will be met with significant domestic and international resistance."

On April 16, Rumsfeld issued his revised menu of "counter-resistance techniques" for interrogators. All the psychological methods were on the list, together with "change of scenery down—removing the detainee from the standard interrogation setting and placing him in a setting that may be less comfortable" and "dietary manipulation"—depriving him of proper meals. All comfort items, including the Koran, could be confiscated. There was no mention of stress positions, but the use of "sleep adjustment" was permitted—this meant "adjusting the sleeping times of the detainee (e.g., reversing sleep cycles from night to day)." With a singular lack of appreciation of the difficulty of sleeping in a metal box without air conditioning during the heat of a Gitmo day, Rumsfeld claimed bizarrely: "This technique is NOT sleep deprivation." Also included was "environmental manipulation: Altering the environment to create moderate discomfort (e.g., adjusting temperature or introducing an unpleasant smell)." This, Rumsfeld acknowledged, would be regarded by some nations as "inhumane."

Finally, and perhaps most important, came isolation in solitary confinement. Rumsfeld placed no limit on the length of time prisoners might have to endure this, but merely commented that it had "not been generally used for interrogation purposes for longer than thirty days." He went on to reveal, in what was then a classified setting, just how cynical was his oft-repeated claim that at Gitmo, America's treatment of detainees was "consistent with the principles" of the Geneva Convention: "Those nations that believe detainees are subject to POW protections may view use of this technique as inconsistent with the requirements of Geneva III." In fact, Rumsfeld admitted, the method breached at least four Geneva articles. But since "the provisions of Geneva are not applicable to the interrogation of unlawful combatants," this was no obstacle.

But for many months to come, the government and its military leaders continued to insist that Gitmo interrogations, like detention conditions there, *were* consistent with the "spirit" of Geneva. It was as if Article 17, with its insistence that prisoners who refused to answer questions shall not be "exposed to unpleasant or disadvantageous treatment of any kind," did not exist. "Guantánamo is a professional, humane, detention and interrogation operation," General James T. Hill of Southern Command in Miami told reporters in June 2004. "It is bounded by law and guided by the American spirit. It has contributed and continues to contribute to winning the war on terror."

I interviewed Shafiq Rasul, Asif Iqbal and Ruhal Ahmed in March 2004, two months before the first public allegations about Abu Ghraib and three before the leak of the memos. Their testimony cannot have been influenced by other media reports. Also in March, the fifth freed British detainee, Jamal al-Harith, gave a long interview to Granada Television and the *Daily Mirror*. Although I did not meet Tarek Dergoul until May, he had, weeks earlier, made the same claims to his London lawyer, Louise Christian. When they were first published, several U.S. government spokesmen denied the prisoners' claims. In the light of the documents quoted above, these rebuttals do not appear credible.

As the pace of interrogations intensified in early 2003, Tarek Dergoul told me, the guards who came to fetch the prisoners began to use a new phrase: "You have a reservation." This did not always mean a prisoner would actually be questioned. For one period of about a month last year, he said, every day guards would take him to an interrogation booth in chains, seat him, chain him to the ring in the floor, and then leave him alone, for eight hours at a time. "The air conditioning would really be blowing, it was freezing, which was incredibly painful on my amputation stumps.

Eventually I'd need to urinate, and in the end I would try to tilt my chair and go on the floor. Inevitably I'd soil myself. It was humiliating. They were watching through a two-way mirror. As soon as I wet myself, a woman MP would come in yelling, 'Look what you've done! You're disgusting.' " Afterward, he would be taken back to his cell for about three hours. Then, he said, the guards would reappear, and the process begin again.

Sometimes, Dergoul said, the interrogators also used heat: "The air-conditioning control would be turned so it was blowing out air even hotter than what was outside. And sometimes, if you budged from your position, they'd take the chair away, so you'd keel over, tipped in agony on to the floor." In periods of especially heavy interrogation, he would be given no clean clothes or bedding, or garments that were too small. Another technique was to refuse toilet paper, "so you can't clean yourself after using the toilet. Or they'd give you like four sheets—not enough to blow your nose."

Asif Iqbal was also left chained in a booth for many hours, and like Dergoul, he was eventually compelled to soil himself. Prisoners were forced to urinate in the booths so often, he said, that it became normal for the interrogators to have their plastic chairs hosed down after each session. Sometimes music would be played at a deafening volume: He remembers having to listen to Eminem, Bruce Springsteen and "techno" dance music, accompanied by flashing strobe lights. Once, he said, an interrogator showed him explicit pornography, saying, "Look at that, it's the last time you'll ever see pussy again." Raised in Britain, he was relatively immune to sexual taunts of this kind: "I just laughed." But Arab detainees told him and Dergoul of being left chained in the booths with their underpants around their ankles, a cause of profound humiliation.

Dergoul also described the use of what was known as the "short shackle," in which the bonds of the three-piece suit were pulled tight to keep the subject bunched up, while chained to the floor. "After a while, it was agony. You could hear the guards behind the mirror, making jokes, eating and drinking, knocking on the walls. It wasn't about trying to get information. It was just about trying to break you." In their letter to the Senate Armed Services Committee, Shafiq Rasul and Asif Iqbal said they too endured this procedure: "We were forced to squat without a chair with our hands chained between our legs and chained to the floor. If we fell over, the chains would cut into our hands. We would be left in this position for hours before an interrogation, during the interrogations (which could last as long as 12 hours), and sometimes for hours while the interrogators left the room. The air conditioning was turned up so high that within minutes we would be freezing. There was strobe lighting and loud music played that was itself a form of torture. Sometimes dogs were brought in to frighten us. We were not fed all the time when we were there, and when we were returned to our cells, we would not be fed that day." Jamal al-Harith told the *Daily Mirror* how "Sometimes you would be chained up on the floor with your hands and feet actually bound together. One of my friends told me he was kept like that for fifteen hours."

In June 2004, *The New York Times* interviewed Parkhudin, a twenty-six-year-old Afghan farmer who was held at Guantánamo from February 2003 to March 2004. He too said that he had been left shackled for hours at a time in uncomfortable positions with a "short chain," adding, "They made me stand in front of an air conditioner. The wind was very cold." It is difficult to disregard so many accounts, notwithstanding Rumsfeld's decision to withdraw permission for the use of "stress positions."

However, it is notable that in the sequence of memos cited above, "stress" techniques always refer to standing. Chaining people on chairs or on the floor, it seems, do not fit this category.

Sleep deprivation (or in Rumsfeld's parlance, "adjustment") was also deployed regularly. Ruhal Ahmed told how the detainees came to speak of "frequent flyers"—prisoners who were forced to don their three-piece suits and move cells, day and night, every two hours. He knew one prisoner, whom he named as Abdul al-Aziz, who endured this for weeks. Tarek Dergoul said the Australian, Mamdouh Habib, had been forced to undergo sleep deprivation to the point where he appeared totally disoriented. Habib—who told Dergoul he had been tortured with electric shocks en route to Guantánamo in Egypt—spoke often of his wife, Malla, and their two children. But he was convinced both were dead, he told Dergoul. Her anguish on learning this after Dergoul's release can only be imagined.

The freed detainees said Gitmo's interrogators used many of the official psychological methods. Among the most common was a claim by an interrogator that he had proof of the suspect's "guilt," a technique that Shafiq Rasul encountered time and again. For example, he was told that photographs of him on an "al-Qaeda membership form" had been found in a raid on an Afghan cave. "Actually I'd left my passport in Pakistan. Then the interrogator told me that next to my file they'd found my brother Habib's al-Qaeda file. The interrogator said he wasn't lying, and that next time he'd bring it with him. When it came to next time, he claimed he'd made a mistake."

Major General Miller's "carrot," the incentives available in return for cooperation, sometimes provoked false allegations by one prisoner against another, which would then become the subject of further intensive interrogation. Shafiq Rasul told me this:

"They kept taking us and taking us saying, 'This guy says you've done this, this guy says you've done that'—what they meant was that other detainees desperate to get out of there were making allegations, making stuff up that they thought would help them get out of the camp." His own interrogators told him the same: "If you want extra comfort items, get us some info on the people on the block." He was asked specifically for incriminating testimony about Jamal al-Harith. "I refused. They said, 'It might help you get out of this place.'" After this session, Rasul said, he was placed on the lowest level regime as a punishment: "You only got a thin mat instead of a mattress, and a blanket only between 11 P.M. and 5 A.M. During the days in the cell you had just your clothes and the Koran."

Asif Iqbal recalled the following: "One inmate said I had been in the al-Farouk terrorist training camp. It led to a whole series of interrogations where they tried to persuade me that I had been. The way the system is, it's accusation after accusation; if this one won't work maybe this one will; if that won't work try this one, until they finally get their confession."

Two months before his release, Rasul's interrogators repeatedly asked him where they could purchase surface-to-air missiles in his home town of Tipton, apparently because another prisoner had claimed he had made such a purchase. (It is striking that in his speech to the Miami Chamber of Commerce, Rumsfeld said that Gitmo had produced valuable information about terrorist acquisitions of these weapons.) As anyone who has visited the quiet British midland town of Tipton would know, it was an absurd suggestion. "I started arguing with him. Did he really think I lived in some sort of war zone? In the beginning I was scared in the interrogations, but toward the end they just seemed stupid."

By the autumn of 2003, the International Committee of the

Red Cross, which continued to visit Gitmo regularly, was becoming intensely concerned about the methods of interrogation and Miller's carrot-and-stick regime. At a meeting in his palm-fringed office on October 9, the minutes of which I have acquired, a Red Cross delegation consisting of Vincent Cassard, Christophe Girod and Thomas Heneke made the organization's strongest protest yet at the treatment of Gitmo's prisoners.

The first matter the Red Cross delegates raised was the fact that they had been unable to see all the detainees. Girod reminded Miller that according to the third Geneva Convention and the "standard operating procedures that they [the Red Cross] follow worldwide," he and his colleagues should be granted "unrestricted access to all areas and to all detainees." Girod, of course, was under the impression that at Gitmo, America was "adhering to the principles" of Geneva. It was to be many months before the text of Bush's order of February 7, 2002, would be declassified, with its caveat that the Convention would be followed only as far as "military necessity" would allow. Miller, however, clearly had read the order. The unseen detainees, he informed Cassard, "were off limits during this visit due to military necessity." ★

Next, Cassard raised the matter of the relentless interrogations, which, he feared, were having serious consequences for the mental health of the detainees. "The I.C.R.C. feels that interrogators have too much control over the basic needs of detainees. That the interrogators attempt to control the detainees through

★ Article 126 of the Convention does allow a detaining power scope to deny access, but only "for reasons of imperative military necessity, and then only as an exceptional and temporary measure." What is envisaged here is refusing access in situations such as a battlefront heading toward a prison camp, not (as Miller seems to have meant) when individuals were being subject to especially rigorous long-term interrogation.

use of isolation . . . that the interrogators have total control of the level of isolation in which the detainees were kept; the level of comfort items detainees can receive; also the access of basic need." Miller did not like to be lectured in this way, declaring he had "issues" with the fact that Cassard had raised the interrogation process at all. "There is no issue with the interrogation methods," he said. "The focus of the I.C.R.C. should be the level of humane detention being upheld, not the interrogation methods. JTF GTMO treats all detainees humanely."

Girod and Cassard took exception to Miller's response. The Red Cross, they said, was focusing "on the psychological pressure and the coercion toward the detainees, and the cumulative effect on their mental health." This was made worse by the fact that there was no legal process that might limit the length of time for which a prisoner was interrogated, and that "here at Guantánamo everything is open ended." Miller shrugged his shoulders, stating that this was a "policy issue, which should be addressed at Washington, D.C."

Yet as the Red Cross delegates began to raise specifics, Miller was put on the defensive and the minutes—produced by his own staff—suggest he simply misled them about the system he himself had created. Possibly he had read *Make 'Em Talk!*, a slim volume by a former military interrogator, Patrick McDonald, who advises his readers the following: "The number one mistake interrogators make when questioning others in ways which could be construed as damaging or offensive is allowing witnesses . . . Remember this if you are faced with legal problems resulting from interrogation you did: deny everything. Admit nothing, and make counter-accusations."

Cassard said he was concerned to see that only those who

cooperated with interrogators received greater privileges, such as transfer to Camp Four. To this, Miller replied, "Every detainee in Camp Delta has the basic elements required by the Geneva Convention. Also, over 85 percent of detainees in Camp Delta get privileges above and beyond basic requirements . . . Does the I.C.R.C. object to these additional privileges?" And, he maintained, privileges were not removed for noncooperation, but "for disciplinary reasons. If a detainee loses a privilege, it is as a result of his actions." Cassard gave the example of interrogators deciding that uncooperative detainees would not be allowed books. Again, Miller's reply was less than the truth: "Restrictions can only occur as a result of detainee disciplinary infractions." Cassard told him that the Red Cross team had heard so many prisoners say that books and other comfort items were confiscated for refusing to talk that they believed this must be true. Miller replied that he would "listen to the allegations but [he had] given the I.C.R.C. the accurate facts."

Coincidentally, my own Guantánamo interview with Major General Miller took place just eight days after he spoke to the Red Cross. As we have seen, with me he made no secret of his belief that subjecting the uncooperative to harsher conditions had boosted the yield of intelligence.

Finally, Cassard complained that medical files about detainees' mental health were being given to interrogators to help them develop "interrogation plans," a practice he described as "a breach of confidentiality between a physician and a patient." In June 2004, *The Washington Post* interviewed numerous officials who confirmed this allegation, including Miller's predecessor, Brigadier General Rick Baccus: The files were "routinely shared with military intelligence personnel," he said, although he was unsure what use they made of them. Had he realized the practice violated rules or international codes, Baccus said, "I would have stopped the process."

Miller adopted a different tactic with the Red Cross: He denied it had happened, advising Cassard and Girod to "check their facts." Their exasperation seeps from the record. "Mr. Cassard raised a concern that Major General Miller was not taking the discussion seriously. Major General Miller explained that he was taking the discussion seriously, that he respected the work and opinions of the I.C.R.C. He also asked the I.C.R.C. team to respect his opinions."

The interrogator who asked Shafiq Rasul how to buy surface-to-air missiles in Tipton was young and inexperienced, like most of those the freed detainees encountered. "You'd look at these guys in their shorts and Polo shirts and think, 'This guy's an interrogator? He's only twenty years old!' " Rasul said.

Gitmo's intelligence troops are organized in five-person groups called "tiger teams," Major General Miller told me, of which seven out of ten were reservists. They were even less well-seasoned than the military intelligence screeners responsible for sending Gitmo its inmates from Afghanistan: Most had come to Camp Delta straight from a course lasting just twenty-five days, which Miller called the "tiger team university" at Fort Huachuca. In most cases, Guantánamo was their very first contact with counterterrorist investigation. Yet Miller claimed their very inexperience was a positive asset: "They're all young people, but they're really committed to winning the mission. Intelligence is a young person's game—you've got to be flexible." He liked to speak to the Fort Huachuca students by videophone before they arrived. "I tell them: The tiger never sleeps at Guantánamo Bay." These young people were so talented and so "committed to winning the mission," that before very long, "our tiger teams will know more about you and your family than you know yourself, and the events that led you into terrorism. We are very, very good at interrogation."

American officers with more experience of intelligence, such as Lieutenant Colonel Christino, who had direct and constant access to Gitmo's "product" in his time at the Pentagon in 2003, do not accept Miller's extraordinary boast. He suggested that inadequate training, as well as inexperience and the reliance on translators put interrogators at a grave disadvantage. "To compare training at Fort Huachuca to a 'university' is a brazen mischaracterization," Christino said. "The 'academic' environment and standards at Fort Huachuca do not compare to those of an accredited university." And until Miller introduced his system of punishment and rewards, Christino pointed out, "interrogators at Guantánamo obtained information of only minimal to moderate intelligence value. Certainly, they gained useful knowledge about recruitment and training, and perhaps some limited insight concerning financing and logistics, but not much about operations. Then along comes Major General Miller and all of a sudden they are producing 'enormously valuable intelligence.' That phrase could only justifiably be applied to detailed information concerning terrorist capabilities and intentions. I doubt that anyone detained at Guantánamo ever had access to that type of information; if some claim that they did, they probably did so to either earn the incentives or avoid the maltreatment that General Miller instituted."

At the same time, assigning such inexperienced staff to interrogate possible terrorists, in almost all cases via interpreters, has not been the way things have been done elsewhere during the war on terror. Dealing with Islamist terrorism since the early 1980s has taught veterans in the CIA and the military many lessons. Among them, said one still-serving intelligence official, is that "it's far more effective to interview a suspect in their own language." So when America seized Abu Zubaydah, said to be one of Osama bin Laden's closest associates, a CIA agent from Kuwait was flown thousands of miles to lead his interrogation. Not only did this agent speak Arabic, he was schooled precisely in the idioms of Abu Zubaydah's local dialect. "Yet they're still using interpreters at Gitmo," the official continued. "What does that tell you? That they don't think the people there are very important. The big guys—Abu Zubaydah, Khalid Shaikh Mohamed [said to be 9/11's operational mastermind]—do you think they're at Gitmo? Of course not."

The preparations interrogators make for interviewing important suspects of this kind are painstaking. "The person who has the advantage is the one who really knows his subject," one specialist of counterterrorist interrogation said. "I would normally spend a minimum of ninety days doing a 'PI,' a preliminary inquiry, on a subject, learning everything about him, before asking a single question. If warranted, I would dig deeper with subpoenas, wiretaps, etc. Sometimes this could even take a year or two before you get to the interview stage." The tiger teams at Gitmo do not operate in this fashion. "I certainly know of no one at Gitmo having the opportunity or the luxury to be able to prepare an interview for three months. Generally, the new hires apprentice in the booths with more experienced guys right from the start. They were rookies."

Guantánamo may even be "a bit of a front," designed to divert al-Qaeda's attention, the first official said. "It takes everybody's attention away from more important matters and locations where 'big fish' are being held. The secrecy surrounding it makes everybody think that very serious stuff is going on there." Multiple sources have confirmed that none of al-Qaeda's known leadership has ever been held at Gitmo. Abu Zubaydah and Khalid Shaikh Mohamed were initially interrogated at a secret location under American control in Thailand, as was 9/11's other principal organizer, Ramzi Binalshibh. Interrogations of confirmed terrorist leaders have also taken place in Pakistan, Jordan and on what one source called "floating interrogation cells" in the Indian Ocean.

The minutes of another meeting at Gitmo between the Red Cross and Major General Miller on February 4, 2004, disclose that as of that date, there was only one detainee out of 652 whose position Miller deemed so sensitive as to deny the Red Cross access—a Moroccan named Abdullah Tabarak, said to have been Osama bin Laden's bodyguard. The closest detainee Gitmo may have to the September 11 attacks is a Saudi named Mohammed al-Kahtani, who was refused entry to the United States at Miami International Airport in August 2001. According to intelligence reports cited by the official 9/11 Commission, he may have been trying to join one of the hijacking teams.

Shafiq Rasul said that in the two years he spent at Gitmo, he met no one he would describe as "hard core." There were, he added, "people who are supposed to be Islamic fundamentalists who don't know how to pray." It is known that one of the prisoners is Abdul Salam Zaeef, former Taliban ambassador to Pakistan, who in an earlier life held regular meetings with American diplomats: In the summer of 2001, with the Taliban enforcing a ban on growing opium, the State Department briefed journalists of the prospects of a rapprochement with the then-Afghan regime and, via Zaeef, was urging the Afghans to expel bin Laden. Days before his arrest in Pakistan in March 2002, Zaeef told reporters that he had "performed his duty in Islamabad as a diplomat," and was not engaged in terrorism. "Still, if there is any suspicion, I am ready to face any open court," he said. In Gitmo, of course, an open court was one of many things he would find unavailable.

As in Afghanistan, most of the Gitmo interpreters are civilians, employed on rolling short-term contracts. And as in Afghanistan, intelligence professionals, including Lieutenant Colonel Christino, expressed grave reservations about the accuracy of their work. One official, a fluent speaker of Arabic, said the almost-universal deployment of interrogations with prisoners at Gitmo who did not speak English undermined any intelligence role Gitmo might have, and had only been possible because of one thing—"the tremendous shortage of qualified Arabists." Most of the "terps" used at Gitmo were "hired expediently, without proper screening." Milton Bearden added, "Getting information from other human beings is hard enough as it is. In my thirty years in the CIA, I guess I've known maybe four or five really good debriefers—I mean people really good at getting information from people who wanted to cooperate. The interrogation of defensive, hostile suspects is obviously far more difficult. And let me tell you: If you have to use interpreters, it just isn't going to work."

As of June 2004, with the former Muslim chaplain James Yee cleared of all security breaches, two men still face serious charges of leaking information from Gitmo to the Middle East. Both worked as terps, and neither appears to have been suitably qualified for the frontline of the war with al-Qaeda. The first man arrested, Ahmad al-Halabi, 23, whose family moved from Syria to the largely Arabic enclave of Dearborn, Michigan, when he was in high school, was sent to Gitmo from a job as a supply clerk at Travis air force base in California, having neither a degree nor any training as a translator. He got the job only because he spoke Arabic at home. Unlike guards or interrogators, who are assigned to Camp Delta with friends as part of a preexisting unit, al-Halabi knew no one, and according to interviews with his family by the *Detroit Free Press,* he felt isolated. His loneliness—and, perhaps, his vulnerability—only intensified when his original three-month tour was twice increased, forcing him to delay his long-planned wedding. As for the second alleged spy, the Egyptian-American Ahmed Fathy Mehalba, he had already tried a military career and failed. As an army private, he had entered the interrogators' school at Fort Huachuca, Arizona, but dropped out because he was overweight. He found himself at Gitmo as an employee of the Titan Corporation of San Diego.

Having exercised staff oversight of contract interpretation and translation services in the Balkans for more than two years, Lieutenant Colonel Christino doubted whether Titan, or any other private sector corporation, was "up to the task of providing the quality of linguists needed to aid in interrogations at Guantánamo." He added that "it takes far more than locating heritage speakers of Arabic within the United States who can obtain an interim security clearance. Unfortunately, that is essentially what the U.S. Army contracted Titan to do. No corporation that I know of keeps a large pool of cleared, professional linguists trained to work with interrogators on retainer."

In early 2003, a group of Pentagon intelligence staff became so concerned about the Gitmo terps that they submitted a memorandum to their civilian bosses, recommending that interrogations should be taped and spot-checked as a means of verifying their work. It was rejected.

"Some good information has come out of Gitmo," one senior Pentagon analyst said. "But it doesn't seem much in relation to the various costs of keeping 600-plus detainees." Christino was more specific: "Most of the information derived from interrogations at Guantánamo appears to be very general in nature; so general that it is not very useful," he said. "How much help is it to know that during a class on improvised explosives at a camp in Afghanistan someone discussed bombing apartment complexes or shopping malls in the United States? Chechen terrorists have been bombing apartment complexes in Russia for years and anyone even vaguely familiar with American consumer culture knows that shopping malls would be a good target."

I asked him to evaluate the bold claims Rumsfeld made in his speech in Miami—that Gitmo interrogations had provided details of terrorist structures, weapons and future plans. "Note how neatly the Secretary's claims fit within the previous discussion of the general nature of most information," he said. "It is quite possible that while undergoing interrogation, a detainee related that an instructor at a training camp in Afghanistan discussed remotely detonating a bomb in a crowded shopping mall. According to the detainee, the instructor maintained that a two-man team, living in an apartment rented by sympathizers in a major American city, could easily do it by constructing an explosive device from materials readily available for retail purchase. The instructor may have even described the type of apartment and the kind of neighborhood and how to accumulate materials through small purchases at different stores around the city—all aimed at not arousing suspicion. Perhaps the detainee went on to describe precisely how to construct and place a remotely detonated bomb. Doesn't that identify details of terrorist structures, weapons and plans? To use Secretary Rumsfeld's vernacular: 'You bet it does.' Is it 'enormously valuable intelligence'? No; it does not identify cities where sympathizers are resident or an execution time frame, so it is not very useful."

Christino pointed out that Mohamed Atta, the principal figure associated with the 9/11 attacks, "was an example of a highly sophisticated terrorist operative outwardly comfortable living in Germany and the United States." He doubted whether many such operatives have ever been detained at Guantánamo. "Most of the detainees are probably not of his breed. It is more likely that they are unsophisticated, fervent Islamist militants who volunteered to defend the Taliban regime and perhaps even bin Laden's al-Qaeda organization from a U.S. attack on Afghanistan."

Christino's assignment as a senior watch officer on the Joint Intelligence Task Force-Combating Terrorism from April until September 2003 happened to be the period when Major General Miller claimed the Gitmo intelligence harvest was at its most bountiful. "During those six months I saw nothing that indicated a dramatic improvement in the quality of intelligence coming from Guantánamo. What I did observe was a major effort at increasing the quantity of intelligence produced and improving the way it was packaged." I asked another seasoned ex-FBI special agent who now works on investigating global terrorist financial networks. "I'm unaware of any important information in my field that's come from Gitmo," he said. "That doesn't mean there's been nothing at all. But it's clearly not a significant source."

Speaking to reporters on a nonattributable basis, Gitmo's supporters have claimed it was responsible for two significant victories in the war against terror: the foiling of a plot to use small boats, laden with explosives, against shipping in the Straits of Gibraltar, and the breakup of a terrorist cell in Milan, Italy. In June 2004, officials who spoke to *The New York Times* questioned those assertions. While some information about Moroccan Islamists had come from Gitmo, any boat attacks were in the "earliest planning stages," *The Times* stated; according to one official, they were only "an idea." As for the disruption of the Italian "logistical cell," Gitmo interrogations had merely helped to confirm information from other sources; to claim the operation as a Gitmo "trophy" would not be accurate.

More candid than his predecessor Geoffrey Miller, the camp's new commandant, Brigadier General Jay W. Hood, acknowledged that expectations about intelligence from Guantánamo "may have been too high."

Lieutenant Colonel Christino's professional critique of the intelligence effort at Guantánamo also includes the interrogation regime run by Major General Miller. In his view, the incentive system Miller created, coupled with the prospect of indefinite detention, makes information obtained through interrogation inherently unreliable. "If a detainee has no hope for release, he is probably going to do whatever he can to improve the quality of his life. Many detainees have spent a year or more locked down under very tough conditions. Offering detainees comfort items, privileges and the promise of eventual transfer to Camp Four in exchange for information is most likely to result in them telling you what they think you want to hear. An incentive system may help control the behavior of detainees but it rarely produces reliable information."

Of course, Gitmo's youthful interrogators also have an array of coercive techniques at their disposal, whose potency they may not fully appreciate. As the case of the three men from Tipton, Ruhal Ahmed, Asif Iqbal and Shafiq Rasul, illustrates, the risk of generating false confessions and other bogus testimony is substantial.

In June 2003, their situation, which had apparently been improving, took a serious turn for the worse. For the previous two weeks, Rasul had been in the relatively comfortable conditions of Camp Four, the lower-security section of Guantánamo where prisoners are freely allowed to associate and play soccer and volleyball. Now, his interrogators told him, American intelligence had acquired a video of a meeting in 2000 between Osama bin Laden and Mohamed Atta, the leader of the 9/11 hijackers. Behind bin Laden were three unidentified men, and someone alleged they were none other than Iqbal, Rasul and Ahmed.

All three were moved to solitary confinement in Camp Delta's isolation block for three months, where the cell walls are made of solid metal instead of mesh, and the only human contact detainees have is with their interrogators. They were to endure this while their interviewers turned on them with a new-found aggression. "The walls were rusty, and they seemed to be soundproofed," Rasul said. "There was no ventilation; it was roasting in there. One interrogator told me that anyone who was in Afghanistan was guilty of the murders of 9/11—even the women and children killed in the American bombing. But they said my position was much worse because the meeting in this video was to plan 9/11, and loads of people had told them that this guy in a beard standing behind bin Laden was me. I told them that in 2000, I didn't leave the country, that I was working at the Wednesbury branch of Curries [a British electronic chain store], who would have my employment records, and attending the University of Central England. They told me I could have falsified those records—that I could have had someone working with me at Curries who could have altered the data the company held, and traveled on a false passport."

Finally, as his isolation continued and the interrogators deployed their full range of techniques, Rasul said, he cracked. In a final session, a senior official had come down from Washington: "My heart is beating, beating, I'm saying it's not me, it's not me, but I'm thinking, 'I'm going to be screwed, I'm on an island in the middle of nowhere, there's nothing I can do.' This woman had come down and she plays me the video. I say, 'Are you blind? That doesn't look anything like me.' But it makes no difference. I'd got to the point where I just couldn't take any more. 'Do what you have to do,' I told them. I'd been sitting there for three months in isolation so I says, 'Yes, it's me. Go ahead and put me on trial.' "

At around the same time, Ahmed and Iqbal made similar confessions. But the three men from Tipton were lucky. Sometime in September 2003, British officials from MI5 came to Guantánamo, armed with the documentary evidence that showed they could not have been in Afghanistan in 2000 after all. Within a few days, they were being held in the ordinary cages again and being given special privileges, including weekly movies in a building known as the "love shack" and hamburgers from the Gitmo McDonald's; a few weeks after that, the American government began to talk to their British counterparts about the men's release. "In the end, we could prove our alibis," Rasul said. "But what about other people, especially from countries where travel records may not be available? What if they confess to something they didn't do and then can't prove it wasn't true?"

The fate of Moazzem Begg, one of the British detainees who was not released in March 2004, may well be an example. Intelligence officials have briefed the American media that after being interrogated at Bagram in Afghanistan for a year, he confessed to planning to drop anthrax spores on the House of Commons from a "drone," an unmanned aerial vehicle. Accurate UAVs are part of the latest generation of American weaponry, and they cost millions of dollars each. Yet in previous reporting of his case, the absurdity of Begg's alleged confession—he supposedly claimed to be plotting to launch his deadly flight from Suffolk—has not been addressed. In one letter to his family, he said he had not seen the sun, sky or stars the entire time he spent at Bagram, where interrogation methods were somewhat harsher than at Gitmo. It does not seem implausible to suggest that his "UAV plot" may have been a fantasy, induced by sheer desperation. I asked a senior Pentagon analyst familiar with the case how much of the evidence against Moazzem Begg depended on his confessions. "A pretty high proportion," he said.

Begg's lawyer, the London solicitor Gareth Peirce, once acted for the defense in three of the most heinous Irish Republican Army terrorism cases: those of the public house bombings in Guildford and Birmingham, in which a total of thirty civilians died in the fall of 1974, and the bombing of a bus on the M62 motorway, which killed ten. (Peirce was played by Emma Thompson in the film *In the Name of the Father,* about the Guildford case.) In all of these examples, the suspects confessed to the police and were sentenced to life imprisonment, reviled by the judges at their trials and the media as embodiments of evil. In each case, fifteen or more years later, conclusive evidence emerged that proved their innocence, and they were exonerated by the Court of Appeal, their lives in tatters. Yet all had been detained for far less time than detainees at Gitmo when they made their bogus confessions—under the English Prevention of Terrorism Act then in force, suspects could be questioned for no more than seven days. Although the six men convicted of the Birmingham bombing were beaten severely by the police, the four people in the Guildford case and Judith Ward, the wrongfully jailed "coach bomber," were subjected only to psychological pressure.

Tom Williamson, formerly the chief of a homicide squad in London's Metropolitan Police and later deputy chief constable of Nottinghamshire, is now a senior research fellow at the Center for Criminal Investigation and Intelligence Studies at Portsmouth University—one of the few places in the world where the science of interrogation is taken seriously. He also holds a doctorate in psychology. "All the research we've done on police interviewing shows that the surest way to get an accurate confession is to have other, reliable evidence, not to put pressure on a suspect," he told me. "If you do turn up the pressure, sure, you will get more confessions, but there will be a very high error rate—in other words, false confessions. In my view, intensive interrogation and torture are not very effective antiterrorist strategies." The big successes that the British had in the latter stages of their war against the I.R.A. stemmed from the successful interception of terrorist communications and the introduction of secret agents into terrorist cells, he said, "and custodial interrogation is no substitute for that kind of effective investigation."

But why do people make false confessions? "For most people," Williamson said, "the tipping point doesn't come with being hooked up to electrodes. It comes much, much earlier. Desperate people will confess to things they haven't done, even though they know it will get them into even deeper trouble. It isn't commonly realized how vulnerable many suspects are. That's why people being interrogated need a lawyer—to stop them saying incriminating things that may not be true, but which happen to make sense to them when they're going through this very bad time."

In his opinion for the Supreme Court in the famous case of *Miranda v. Arizona,* Chief Justice Earl Warren made the same point: "It is not just the subnormal or woefully ignorant who succumb to an interrogator's imprecations, whether implied or expressly stated, that the interrogation will continue until a confession is obtained," he said.

Perhaps the world's leading authority on false confessions is Professor Gisli Gudjonsson, of London's Institute of Psychiatry, the author of several works on the subject and a veteran of dozens of cases in which he has testified as an expert witness. After many years of research, summarized in his 2003 book *The Psychology of Interrogations and Confessions,* he finds that certain personality types are more prone to making untrue admissions, and that the greater the means brought to "overbear the subject's will," the greater the risk of generating false testimony. Even the "ordinary" psychological methods used routinely by American police and set out in the standard military intelligence Field Manual 34-52, such as good cop, bad cop and "we know all," can be very risky. When combined with more rigorous techniques such as sleep deprivation, isolation, exposure to cold or shackling in "stress positions," the dangers are much greater. Citing the example of Americans captured in the Korean War, when hundreds confessed and begged to atone for "crimes" they had not committed, Gudjonsson notes that their Communist captors "exploited human vulnerabilities and weaknesses that had been induced or exacerbated by fatigue, sleep deprivation, insufficient or inadequate diet, uncertainty, pain and general physical discomfort." One of the most potent tools, he adds, was "placing subjects in a situation from which there is no escape," when a combination of mental and physical stress "result in a state of confusion so that the prisoner is unable to distinguish between what is true and what is untrue."

I asked Gudjonsson about Gitmo. He told me this: "The longer people are detained, the harsher their conditions and the worse their lack of any support system, the greater the risk that what they say will be unreliable. What I have found striking over the years is the confidence that police officers and prosecutors have in their ability to tell when someone is guilty. Sometimes I'm asked to look at these cases. There's been a confession, sometimes even on videotape, but I find myself less confident. And then, out of the blue, a DNA sample proves they were innocent all along. There is a belief that once you have a confession, you have the right person. The first thing any interrogator should acknowledge is you may well get a false confession from someone who is vulnerable, and it's a lot easier than most people think."

Of course, history provides many examples of false confessions by the victims of treatment that falls far short of the extreme measures described in the August 2002 Department of Justice memo, with its insistence that true torture must be defined as "equivalent in intensity to the pain accompanying serious physical injury, such as organ failure, impairment of bodily function, or even death." None of the innocents executed after Stalin's show trials pleaded not guilty, and all confessed. Between 1935 and 1939, writes Gudjonsson, between 5 and 10 percent of the entire Soviet population was arrested. "The extraction of confessions functioned to justify these arrests and was intended to reassure the public of these persons' guilt . . . interrogations were typically carried out at night and combined beatings, extensive sleep-deprivation, deprivation of social contact, physical discomfort, threats and intimidation." Many later died in the *gulag,* but few, if any, died while providing their interrogators the answers that would cause them to be sent there.

In his book cited at the head of this chapter, Sir Keith Thomas writes that despite the thousands burned at the stake in the great European witch-hunts, "ritual devil worship was probably a myth," an idea derived entirely from fictitious confessions. Matthew Hopkins, England's brilliantly successful seventeenth-century Witchfinder General, relied mainly on sleep and food deprivation: "It was no accident that he was more successful than anyone else in extracting confessions of devil worship." Like the frustrated Gitmo interrogators who asked Major General Miller to seek authorization to expand their repertoire of techniques to "counter resistance," Hopkins's master, James I, believed that tougher methods were required to produce confessions from those with the most to hide. "Loathe they are to confess without torture," he wrote in his *Daemonologie.* "This in itself, witnesseth their guilt."

None of us can read men's minds. Absent decisive corroboration, the only way to determine whether an admission extracted after months of questioning from a Gitmo prisoner that he once met with Mohamed Atta and Osama bin Laden happens to be true, is the process that intelligence officers call "analysis": cross-checking a statement's contents with databases and other known facts. There is an analyst on every "tiger team" at Gitmo, and it may not surprise the reader to discover that Major General Geoffrey Miller was typically effusive about their abilities. "False confessions or other testimony may occur in some very remote circumstances," he said. "But I believe that we understand what the truth is. Some detainees are not honest to begin with, and I'm very conscious of the risk of gathering false stories. But our tiger teams will spend months investigating you and your background. They're not only investigating the how of terrorism, but the why. They can identify the truth of any statement made with a high degree of accuracy."

In which case, it could be said, it is somewhat surprising that they did not spot the lack of truth in Shafiq Rasul's confession, instead accusing him of having falsified the 2002 employment records that showed he was selling personal stereos and televisions in Wednesbury not meeting with Osama bin Laden in Afghanistan.

Once again, Lieutenant Colonel Christino supplied a sense of perspective: "Our analytical capability is inadequate, whether in Guantánamo or elsewhere, because there are very few people with sufficient training and experience to properly cull through good and bad information." Having access to databases was all very well, he said. However, they already contained a lot of inaccurate information, which sharply reduced their effectiveness. And as in Afghanistan, there was a strong disposition to be credulous: "The interrogators and analysts want to make a contribution, and that makes them want to believe that these detainees are dangerous terrorists. I think that it is very difficult for our people to accept that many of the detainees simply may have been Islamic-oriented guerrilla fighters in the decades-long conflict in Afghanistan. It is probably infinitely harder for them to accept that someone sent to Guantánamo may not have had any malevolent connection to either al-Qaeda or the Taliban regime." Milton Bearden made a related point. Gitmo interrogations, he suggested, were "driven by ideology—the need to justify the detentions themselves—rather than by what intelligence agencies have learnt are effective means of extracting information from people." Miller and Rumsfeld claimed that all of the Gitmo detainees were terrorists or supporters of terrorism. One of the interrogators' prime tasks was to produce the evidence to "prove" they were right.

Throughout the developed world, aware of the difficulty of distinguishing true statements from false, judges and lawmakers have tried to establish a less daunting standard for determining whether to accept prisoners' confessions: whether they were voluntary, freely given. This was the central issue for the Supreme Court justices in *Miranda v. Arizona*. "This Court has recognized that coercion can be mental as well as physical, and that the blood of the accused is not the only hallmark of an unconstitutional inquisition," Chief Justice Earl Warren wrote. Police interrogators were trained to use tactics "designed to put the subject in a psychological state where his story is but an elaboration of what the police purport to know already—that he is guilty. Explanations to the contrary are dismissed and discouraged. It is obvious that such an interrogation environment is created for no purpose other than to subjugate the individual to the will of his examiner."

He could have been describing the Gitmo booths, although there, the duration and intensity of the pressure applied is many times greater. According to Warren, the Fifth Amendment, and the protection it provides against a prisoner being compelled to incriminate himself, was "one of this Nation's most cherished principles." Of course, before the Supreme Court ruled at the end of June 2004 that Gitmo detainees were covered by the U.S. Constitution and could file suit in American courts, the involuntariness of their confessions had barely been considered, at least inside the Pentagon. The series of memos in which the administration set out the policies quoted above explicitly state that the Fifth Amendment did not apply at Guantánamo.

But involuntary the confessions certainly were. On June 13, 2004, the Reuters news wire carried a statement by Colonel Jerry Cannon, head of Gitmo's Joint Detention Group, concerning the Extreme Reaction Force discussed in chapter two and the tapes that exist of its deployment: "Forty-five percent of the [500 hours of videotapes] of ERFs are ones who don't want to go to interrogations," Cannon said. "Sometimes you've got to carry them all the way." He denied claims that some detainees had suffered broken bones in this process, but confirmed that others had been subjected to pepper sprays. The products of interrogations conducted after such incidents would probably not, it is fair to say, meet the Supreme Court's standards in *Miranda v. Arizona*.

4

THE MEANINGS OF GUANTÁNAMO BAY

Words had to change their ordinary meanings and to take that which was now given them.
—Thucydides, *History of the Peloponnesian War*

In the case of a word like democracy, *not only is there no agreed definition, but the attempt to make one is resisted from all sides. It is almost universally felt that when we call a country democratic we are praising it: consequently the defenders of every kind of regime claim that it is a democracy, and fear that they might have to stop using that word if it were tied down to any one meaning.*
—George Orwell, *Politics and the English Language*

For Shafiq Rasul, Asif Iqbal and Ruhal Ahmed, the end of their Guantánamo stay came unexpectedly, and like so much they had endured, as the result of arbitrary decisions by distant powers. Several weeks after the international media, they were told they were going to be freed and to prepare themselves for travel. "They took us to the airport in chains," Rasul said, "and when we got there this huge plane was surrounded by armed men. As we walked towards the steps they had guns trained on us. This military police guy hands us over to the British, takes off our shackles and tells the Brit he can put on the handcuffs. But the British policeman says, 'No, no, there's no need for handcuffs.' We walk up the steps and they're not even touching me. For the first time in two years I'm walking somewhere without being frog-marched. We get to the door and someone says, 'Good morning. Welcome aboard.' "

Returning to London, they were questioned at Paddington Green police station. But this time, they had attorneys present and were not chained. To no one's surprise, the Scotland Yard anti-terrorist branch was unable to find evidence they had any link with terrorism. They were free—though not to return to their homes in Tipton, a stronghold of the extreme right wing British National Party, where effigies of men in orange jumpsuits had been hung from lampposts in the days before their return.

Nor had they escaped the false accusations. In the week after their release, the tabloid *Sun* newspaper published claims by a U.S. Embassy spokesman, Lee McClenny, who said that they had, after all, trained at an al-Qaeda camp in 2000, notwithstanding the fact that MI5 had already proved that none of them left the United Kingdom that year. Afterward, I tried to call McClenny several times, but he refused to come to the telephone. Lieutenant Colonel Sumpter, the Gitmo public affairs spokesman, said any allegations concerning detainees were highly classified, even after their release: "I don't know how the Embassy got this. It didn't come from us, and we knew nothing about it." McClenny's statement was also disowned by the State Department. It was not going to be easy for the freed detainees to return to domestic obscurity, let alone paid employment.

For more than two years, the United States had imposed a

warped and largely imaginary version of reality on them, at enormous human cost. This is Gitmo's first meaning: the shattering of innocents' lives, and for detainees' families, an indeterminate sentence of uncertainty and loss. In a fifth-floor walk-up council flat in Maida Vale, not far from the police station where Rasul and his friends spent their last hours in captivity, I met Jeanette Belmar, whose brother Richard remained at Gitmo when the first five British detainees were released in March 2004. She told me that Richard, who was born in October 1979, had not been a success at school and found it hard to settle in life, until, at the age of sixteen, he converted to Islam. "After that I saw a change in him. He seemed calmer, more focused; no longer worried about needing to have the latest clothes and fashions." Richard traveled to Pakistan in June 2001 to study the Koran at a religious school. He kept in touch with his family by telephone, and after 9/11, he told them he was on his way back. And then: Silence, for more than a year, until mid-October 2002, when his father received a phone call from the Foreign Office, saying Richard was at Guantánamo.

"It's hard enough to go to work and try to be an ordinary person and forget that this is happening," she said. "But as soon as I walk through the door back home, we don't talk or think about much else. You turn on the TV news and you see stories about people around the world in much worse situations than us. That's one way you try to stay positive: I know my brother, and I know that's what he would want me to do. But . . ." she trailed off, her eyes welling. "I don't hold a grudge against Americans. Please don't think that. It's their government."

She showed me a letter written by Richard from Pakistan in September 2001. It talked about a rigorous regime of prayer and study, and aside from the fact that its envelope bore a Pakistani stamp and postmark, it did not appear to describe the Afghan terrorist training camp that American officials told *The Daily Telegraph* Belmar had been attending. More poignant were two from Camp Delta: "Don't forget me Jeanette," he wrote in June 2003. "I love you and I miss you. Insh'allah [God willing] we'll meet again." The second was dated September 18, 2003. "What's up Jeanette?" it began, in an apparent attempt to be breezy. "How are you doing? I wish I could be saying 'salaam aleikum' [greetings] to you. I hope one day insh'allah I will." Its ending was more worrying, suggesting he was slipping into delusion: "I have had a few dreams of me being released, and other people have seen things too." This was the last message the family had received—nine months earlier at the time we met.

Could Belmar have been a terrorist, involved (as Dick Cheney put it) in plots to kill thousands of ordinary Americans? If so, he had not had much time to make connections or learn his skills. A few weeks after meeting Jeanette, I spoke with a seasoned U.S. official who had interviewed Belmar after his arrest—in Pakistan, not on any "battlefield." Like so many others, he said, Belmar had merely been "swept up." The official told me that he had recommended his immediate release. Shortly afterward, Belmar was flown to Guantánamo.

Tears have been shed by countless others, in more than forty countries. Rabiye Kurnaz, from Bremen, Germany, told me that soon after her son Murad, then nineteen, was sent to Gitmo in January 2002, she received two postcards, but nothing in the more than two years since. "He was almost a child. We know you can write, but he doesn't. He's the only German speaker there and he speaks neither English nor Arabic."

The number of children left without fathers must be well

into five figures. Four are Moazzem Begg's, the youngest of whom he has never seen, being brought up by his wife Sally in Birmingham. "When I first came home [after his capture] I broke down and cried," she told the local *Evening Mail.* "I could not stay in our house and I still break down. When he was taken to Guantánamo Bay I had already heard of torture there. He wrote to say he didn't know why he was there and that he needed help but didn't know where to get it. Another time his letter started: 'My beloved wife and children.' I could not read any more. He is missing his children's childhood. We are alone and my heart breaks when every time the doorbell rings Marium runs to answer it, always sure it is her father—and it never is. And then, at bed time, she cries herself to sleep. He kept saying 'I just want to come home' in his letters. I want him home, here, in our house. But even then I won't be happy. I know he will be mentally unstable and I will not be able to understand him, because however he explains it, I have not been through what he has been through; how can I ever help, ever really understand?"

Replicated across the Muslim world, the anguish of Gitmo detainee families has tapped new veins of anti-American rage. "The guy with the crewcut, the club and the crucifix, standing over the detainee in goggles and chains, symbolizes not only American oppression of the Third World, but also the oppression by governments friendly to America inside Muslim countries," said Dr. Tim Winter, lecturer in Islamic studies at Pembroke College, Cambridge. "People's instinct is to emphasize with the guy in the goggles because that's how they see the world." According to Winter, a frequent visitor to the Middle East and fluent in Arabic, "Guantánamo is right up there with the Palestinian conflict as a focal point for anger and political action."

"The lawlessness of the U.S. is a projection of the unsavory ferocity of the global hyper-power and a legacy of the neo-conservatives that run the White House," says a recent editorial in Britain's (politically moderate) *Muslim News,* which has published several long features about Guantánamo. "Out of the window has gone any regard for the norms of international law and order . . . with Muslims liable to be kidnapped in any part of the world to be transported to Guantánamo Bay and face summary justice." A senior Defense Intelligence Agency official admitted: "It's an international public relations disaster. Maybe the guy who goes into Gitmo does so as a farmer who got swept along and did very little. He's going to come out a fully-fledged jihadist. And for every detainee, I'd guess you create another ten terrorists or supporters of terrorism."

On Islamist websites and in the Arab press, Guantánamo is cited time and again as a rallying point for jihad, as a justification for creating more suicide "martyrs." At the time of writing, terrorism has discovered a new vogue: The decapitation of western hostages in Iraq and Saudi Arabia, videotaped before and during their executions in orange costumes, in deliberate imitation of the detainee uniform at Gitmo.

Since January 2002, the rhetoric of Donald Rumsfeld and President Bush has reinforced the message of those first, shocking photographs: that the detainees were in some way subhuman, lacking the qualifications for full membership of the species; *untermenschen.* For the military lawyer Lieutenant Commander Charles Swift, assigned to defend Osama bin Laden's erstwhile driver Salim Ahmed Hamdan at a Gitmo military commission on conspiracy charges, the inadequacy of that characterization was palpable when he entered his new client's cell for the first time.

"Here was not just a detainee but a human being. He had lovely children, and he showed me their photographs; and a wife who was worried sick about him. And he had a defense: Like many Yemenis, in 1995 he went to work outside Yemen because there was no work there and he needed a job. As far as he was concerned, Osama bin Laden was just a rich Saudi from a rich and famous family who needed drivers—Salim was one of five that he employed. He always considered himself a civilian employee— never a member of al-Qaeda or the Taliban."

After being charged in 2004, Hamdan, together with five other detainees designated eligible for trial, including the Australian David Hicks and the Britons Moazzem Begg and Feroz Abassi, was moved to a new, locked-down, permanent isolation facility outside Camp Delta's gates, Camp Echo. According to the freed detainees, a few men have returned thence to the main Guantánamo camp, describing a white-walled, sound-absorbent hell of 24-hour solitary confinement in cells still smaller than Camp Delta's, with a guard permanently stationed outside each cell door. At first, the only times Hamdan was allowed out of his cell was to exercise at night.

In March 2004, Swift filed a federal suit in Seattle, challenging the conditions of Hamdan's detention and key aspects of the military commission trial process. Accompanying it was an affidavit from Professor Daryl Matthews, the forensic psychiatrist (see chapter two) who examined Gitmo's prisoners at the behest of the Pentagon. Hamdan, Matthews wrote, was "deteriorating" in Camp Echo, and he had experienced "frustration, rage (although he has not been violent), loneliness, depression, despair, anxiety, and emotional outbursts." Swift told Matthews his meetings with his client usually ended with Hamdan begging him not to leave. According to Matthews: "Mr. Hamdan's current conditions of confinement place him at significant risk for future psychiatric deterioration, possibly including the development of irreversible psychiatric symptoms." They also make him extremely likely to make a false confession.

There was another reason for Hamdan's bleak mood, Swift told me. "When he was first charged he was pleased, because it meant that at last, he was getting a hearing. Then I had to tell him that the way the system worked, the best that might happen if he won would not be that he'd be released, but that he'd just go back to Camp Delta. That left him in tears." Even if found not guilty, Gitmo's unlawful enemy combatants would stay where they were, in Donald Rumsfeld's words, to "keep them off the streets." In February 2004, Pentagon officials briefed reporters that in some cases, detainees might be convicted of crimes by the military commissions, serve their sentences, and then continue to be held indefinitely because they were still deemed too dangerous to release. Some, it was claimed, "remain committed to indiscriminately killing American civilians and soldiers."

When the military commission rules were first published in 2003, they provoked outrage among lawyers. There would be no such thing as attorney-client privilege, the rules said, because conversations between a defendant and his lawyer might be bugged. The official reason for holding prisoners in Camp Echo, which Miller explained to the Red Cross delegation at the meeting (see chapter three) on October 9, 2003, is thus somewhat curious: "Camp Echo is an appropriate facility that allows detainees to have private conversations with their lawyers." As so often with Guantánamo, however, there seems to have been a secret, truer reason behind the Potemkin façade. "Returning Mr. Hamdan to the general facility would create a grave harm to the environment the military is creating to gain intelligence to fight the war against al-Qaeda," assistant solicitor-general Gregory Garre told the Seattle court where Swift filed his petition. What could this possibly be? The *Seattle Post-Intelligencer* reported, "A government source said Garre was referring to a concern that Hamdan's fellow prisoners, none of whom have lawyers, might stop talking to interrogators if they learn that he has an attorney."

It was a revealing comment, with hidden layers of significance. If the United States and its Constitution stand for anything, it is the ambition expressed by the Enlightenment: The replacement of absolutist monarchy with codified, rational, legally answerable government, derived from Montesquieu's doctrine of the separation of powers, and with a further separation between church and state. The exercise of power was not to be limitless and was to be invigilated by the courts. Yet here was an American official stating without irony that prisoners must be held in cruel and indefinite isolation lest their fellow detainees, who might still be coerced into incriminating themselves, should ascertain they had lawyers. What could account for it?

At one level, this was simply a function of the denial of legal rights at Gitmo and the government's insistence that alien non-U.S. citizens had no rights there. But consigning prisoners to the legal black hole of Guantánamo reflected a broader sense of their dehumanization, an inferior status that made them undeserving of a normal enemy's privileges; a status that was not based on evidence of what they had done, but who they were. With most members of the Bush Administration, these attitudes have to be inferred, but one senior Pentagon official directly responsible for Guantánamo has come close to voicing them outright—Lieutenant General William G. Boykin, Deputy Undersecretary for Intelligence.

Like Major General Miller, Boykin had no experience in intelligence before assuming this post, which put him personally in charge of the hunt for bin Laden and the Taliban leader Mullah Omar. Boykin is a Christian fundamentalist, who has preached church sermons in which he has stated the superiority of Christianity over Islam and the divine nature of America's mission in the war on terror.

President Bush, he told a church in Maryland, had been anointed by God: "Why is George W. Bush in the White House? . . . You must recognize that we as Americans saw a miracle unfold with the election of George W. Bush. Whether you voted for him or not is irrelevant. The fact is he is there today not only to lead America, but to lead the world, and that is what he is doing. Where does he start his day? He starts his day in the Oval Office at 4:30 with a Bible in his hand." To those who accused him of blurring the separation of church and state, Boykin retorted: "If you don't believe that this nation was founded on Christian beliefs, Christian values, then go back and read the writings and the orations of the founders of this nation, read what they said. Every man that signed the Constitution of the United States was of the Christian faith."

In June 2003, Boykin preached to a congregation in Oregon, wearing his full dress uniform, and claimed that radical Islamists hated the United States "because we're a Christian nation, because our foundation and our roots are Judeo-Christian," while "the enemy is a guy named Satan." Terrorists, he said, came from the "principalities of darkness" and were "demonic." Discussing a battle he once fought against a Muslim warlord in Somalia,

Boykin said he had been confident of victory because "I knew my God was bigger than his. I knew that my God was a real God and his was an idol."

There are precedents in American history for stratifying humanity in this fashion, such as those moments in the nineteenth century when the Supreme Court forgot the motto inscribed above its portal: "Equal Justice under Law." In *Dred Scott v. Sandford* (1857) the court ruled that African Americans, slaves as well as free, could never be U.S. citizens; in *Plessey v. Ferguson* (1896) it upheld the oppression of Jim Crow segregation.

Gitmo has another resonance that is perhaps less well known. In 1862, while the Civil War raged farther south, the Dakota Sioux rebelled and attacked white settlers. General John Pope, sent by President Lincoln to crush the revolt, approached his mission with a bloodthirsty zeal, declaring: "It is my purpose to utterly exterminate the Sioux . . . They are to be treated as maniacs or wild beasts, and by no means as people with whom treaties or compromise can be made." This was not the rhetoric of Gettysburg or Emancipation, but of the conquistadors: Pope was a subscriber to the doctrine of "manifest destiny," which held that Christian America's westward expansion was justified by divine right, and that this encompassed a moral duty to subjugate or slaughter the "Red Man" who lay in its wake.

Defeating the Sioux in battle, Pope took almost 400 prisoners and subjected them to summary trial by military commission—so summary that they had neither lawyers nor any opportunity to present evidence in their defense. Indeed, Pope wrote later, "the degree of guilt was not one of the objects to be attained" by the commissions, for it "would have been impossible" to devote enough time to establish the details of so many cases. He was satisfied, however, "that at least seven-eighths of those sentenced to be hung have been guilty of the most flagrant outrages and many of them concerned in the violation of white women or the murder of children." In this fashion, 303 were condemned to death, although Lincoln eventually commuted all but 38 of these sentences.

As the former military lawyer Donald Rehkopf, now a civilian involved in Guantánamo defense, noted in a paper for his fellow attorneys, "Under present definitions, the Sioux would clearly be 'terrorists,' a linguistic revision of their then status as 'savages.' " It is a matter of record that the U.S. Army refused to treat the Sioux as prisoners of war. Like their distant successors at Guantánamo, they were classed as "unlawful combatants."

Not even General Boykin has ever gone so far as to claim that Gitmo detainees deserve to be treated as savages or wild beasts. But their categorization as unlawful enemy combatants was part of a much more general retreat from American constitutional norms and the values of the Enlightenment. At Gitmo, at the war on terror's other detention facilities in Iraq and Afghanistan, and in the convoluted set of reasons the government's lawyers set down to justify the use of torture, the Bush Administration was not seeking to modify old rules in order to accommodate them to a new kind of war, but to jettison them and to replace them with a system governed by a single principle—that because America and its President were fighting a just war, whatever they might find expedient would be right. This was not evolution, but a violent rupture. It suggested that Bush's Texan Republicanism belonged among the messianic ideologies of the twentieth century, with their insistence that desirable ends would justify necessary means.

The clearest statements of this principle are contained in the memos cited in chapter three concerning interrogation methods and torture. In another related context, that of the opposition expressed by France and Germany to a preemptive and, in their view, illegal war in Iraq, Donald Rumsfeld was to speak with contempt of "old Europe." But old Europe and its philosophers—whose ideas informed the young American republic—had long ago condemned the use of torture, and identified its moral and practical shortcomings. As Montesquieu saw that the best way to build a defense against despotism was to separate the executive, legislative and judicial branches of government, so he recognized that torture is the means by which an unrestrained executive maintains itself. (*Vide,* in the epoch of George W. Bush, Saddam Hussein's Iraq.)

Cesare Beccaria realized that torture is not only repugnant, it doesn't "work," in the sense of providing discernibly accurate information. "The only difference between torture and trials by fire and boiling water is, that the event of the first depends on the will of the accused, and of the second on a fact entirely physical and external: but this difference is apparent only, not real," he wrote in his *On Crimes and Punishments* in 1764. "A man on the rack, in the convulsions of torture, has it as little in his power to declare the truth, as, in former times, to prevent without fraud the effects of fire or boiling water." The greater the pressure, the less reliable the testimony: "The very means employed to distinguish the innocent from the guilty will most effectually destroy all difference between them." As a means of gathering what at Gitmo might be termed "enormously valuable" intelligence, torture was equally ineffective: "Torture is used to make the criminal discover his accomplices; but if it has been demonstrated that it is not a proper means of discovering truth, how can it serve to discover the accomplices, which is one of the truths required? Will not the man who accuses himself yet more readily accuse others?" Beccaria found it amazing that rulers were still employing torture in the late eighteenth century. The evidence against it was so strong, it seemed extraordinary that mankind still "neglected to draw the obvious conclusion."

In old Europe, even despots could be enlightened. Frederick the Great of Prussia had banned torture even before Beccaria's book, in 1754. Its publication is generally held responsible for abolition in Baden (1767), by Gustavus II of Sweden (1772), Louis XIV of France (1780), Joseph II of Austria (1781), and Leopold of Tuscany (1786). By the end of the nineteenth century, torture was extinct both in Europe and North America. As Neil Belton notes in *The Good Listener,* his book about human rights and Helen Bamber, founder of the Medical Foundation for the Care of Victims of Torture where Tarek Dergoul became a patient after leaving Guantánamo, the 1914 edition of the *Encyclopaedia Britannica* declared the following: "The whole subject [of torture] is now one of only historical interest, as far as Europe is concerned." It was, of course, about to make a terrible comeback.

Modern experts, both psychologists and spies, have accepted the truth of Beccaria's insights. "It is obvious torture may produce false testimony from the innocent," Professor Gisli Gudjonsson, the specialist on the psychology of confessions, told me. "At the same time, there's no research that suggests that it produces accurate information from the guilty." Milton Bearden, formerly of the CIA, concurred. "I spent quite a bit of time during my career advising governments who were using such techniques, 'No, no, that's not how we do it.' Ultimately, the purpose of torture is torture. The way you *do* get information from people is through a process that amounts to recruitment, by doing deals." Sometimes, said a veteran FBI special agent, such recruitments might take place when "you have a hammer to hold over them"—not the threat or reality of inflicting pain, but a piece of information. More often, he had "flipped" witnesses by taking pains to build trust and rapport.

Yet running through the government lawyers' memoranda, starting with Jay S. Bybee's paper at the Department of Justice on August 1, 2002, is an unspoken assumption: Torture, and the less extreme coercive methods that would not quite meet torture's definition, must be the ideal way to pry information from those taken captive in the war on terror. The same assumption was reflected in the requests for permission to use tougher methods made by Gitmo's frustrated interrogators later that year, and in the system Major General Miller eventually instituted there and at Abu Ghraib. Like the inquisitors of pre-Enlightenment Europe, they seem to have believed—bereft, as they were, of the least experience of gathering useful intelligence—that confessions produced by torture and coercion would be the "queen of proofs."

The lawyers also shared a delusion common among advocates of torture in order to combat terrorism—the legend of the "ticking bomb," the hypothetical case where a terrorist is captured after planting an explosive device, but before its detonation. (After 9/11, exactly such a scenario was popularized by the television series *24,* in which the good guys torture a terrorist without a qualm.) Here Alan Dershowitz of Harvard University anticipated even Bybee, advocating torture in such instances in articles in the *Los Angeles Times* and elsewhere as early as November 2001. With estimable respect for the rule of law, Dershowitz's only proviso was that such torture should not be administered in secret, but by judicial warrant.

The ticking bomb legend informed the Israeli commission led by Moshe Landau, which authorized the general use of stress positions, hooding, sleep deprivation and other methods by Shin Bet against Palestinian suspects in the Occupied Territories. In none of the thousands of recorded cases where suspects were abused in this manner was there ever such a bomb.★ The legend also informed Bybee's memo, and its proposal that an American accused of torture could use the defenses of necessity or self-defense: "Al-Qaeda plans apparently include efforts to develop and deploy chemical, biological and nuclear weapons of mass destruction. Under these circumstances, a detainee may possess information that could enable the United States to prevent attacks that potentially could equal or surpass the September 11 attacks in their magnitude. Clearly, any harm that might occur during an interrogation would pale into insignificance compared to the harm avoided by preventing such an attack." Bybee accepted that applying this argument would depend on circumstances: The more certain interrogators were that a suspect did possess such knowledge, the stronger such a defense to claims of torture would be. But like others who have explored this moral swamp,

---

★ In the extensive research he conducted for his *The Good Listener,* Neil Belton came across only one example where the ticking bomb scenario had actually materialized: an incident in Algeria in 1956, when the police caught a Communist placing a bomb near a gas container and feared a second had already been planted. The police wanted to torture the suspect, but Paul Teitgen, the prefecture secretary-general, refused. "I trembled the whole afternoon," Teitgen later told the writer Alistair Horne. "Finally the bomb did not go off. Thank God I was right. Because once you get into the torture business, you are lost . . . All our civilization is covered with a varnish."

he did not pause to examine the case that corresponds more closely with reality: The captive who *might* know something about terrorism, even a deadly and imminent attack—but, equally, might not.

In order to permit coercive interrogations at Guantánamo, the administration had to make further inroads into the principles expressed by the U.S. Constitution. Its other target was due process, and its insistence that evidence should only be admitted into criminal proceedings if properly gathered; that trials must be open, and justice seen to be done; and that verdicts should be subject to independent judicial review. Bush and his government had, in other words, to ensure that the tribunals by which Gitmo's prisoners were tried were only slightly fairer than those employed by General Pope against the Sioux.

The interrogation techniques and the rules for the conduct of military commissions did not arise in isolation: one was a corollary of the other. "You could justify the interrogations, and indeed the whole Gitmo process, by pointing to the fact that the authors of confessions had been convicted of terrorist crimes," said Lieutenant Commander Swift, Salim Hamdan's military lawyer. "Interrogations could be coercive because the commission rules allowed the methods used to stay secret, and they were almost unchallengeable anyway. But now they're stuck, because the techniques, which were supposed to stay classified, have come out into the open." (It might also be said that the Pentagon's legal establishment led by general counsel William Haynes had not reckoned on the defense counsel it assigned to Gitmo turning out to be individuals of the courage and caliber of Charlie Swift.)

Naturally, the commission rules make no provision for excluding a confession exacted through duress; nor is there any protection against hearsay. Indeed, a Gitmo commission could consider anything that a "reasonable person" might find of probative value, while the prosecution could use secret evidence from intelligence sources that a defendant would not even be allowed to hear. Unlike laws in regular courts, the commission rules also changed several times in response to political pressure. For example, when he wished to make things easier for the Australian prime minister John Howard, who had supported his policy in Iraq, President Bush agreed that unlike other defendants, the Australian David Hicks could be represented by a foreign, civilian lawyer, and he could phone his family.

It was true, Lieutenant Colonel Fred Borch, the lead prosecutor, told me, that the absence of any rules of evidence gave the officers who made up a commission a vast discretion, placing a huge burden on them to ensure that trials were fair—as the Pentagon insists they would be. "The only way to achieve that is through having people of high integrity," he said. "Why don't you wait until we have our first case? And then I think in the end you are going to be convinced that it is a fair proceeding and we have done the right thing." Major Michael Shavers, the commissions' spokesman, said much the same thing: Trials would be just, because "good people" would be conducting them. I heard the same message several times from others in the Pentagon. Reduced to essentials, it came down to two words: "Trust us."

Yet the essence of the rule of law, summarized by the motto at the gates of Harvard law school, is "not under man but God and the law." A tradition reaching back to Magna Carta and beyond suggests that relying on the goodness of individuals is a very weak basis for delivering justice. *The Uniform Code of Military Justice,* the lawbook for courts martial, has long recognized this difficulty. In recognition of human fallibility, even where members of the American military are concerned, one of the standard claims the code allows in appeals filed by military convicts is that the original trial was flawed by "unlawful command influence"—that members of a military jury were picked by the same officer who would later write their annual appraisal, for example. Of course, military convicts may appeal their cases to civilian judges. Under the system as originally envisioned, Guantánamo prisoners would have had no such recourse. Their highest appeal would have been to the commander in chief, President Bush, whose public statements might be said to have equated to precisely this kind of command influence. To have granted an appeal, he would have had to repudiate his own statements, such as one he made in 2003 when the British prime minister Tony Blair criticized the commission rules: "I know for certain these are bad people."

The commissions had the power to award the death penalty, without even the necessity for unanimity among the seven officers who would be needed to hear a capital case. As governor of Texas, Bush presided over 152 executions, more than any governor in American history. The commission rules gave him the same power of life and death at Gitmo.

We need to see Gitmo not as a discrete phenomenon, but as a large component in a revolutionary system, in which the administration was mounting attacks on two pillars of both the Enlightenment and the Constitution—on their retreat from torture, and on due process. They were only made possible by a third legal assault, against the separation of powers. Running through the entire documentary record of the war on terror is a single theme: The unlimited power of the American president to override treaties, conventions and laws in time of war. The argument was made on January 9, 2002, by John Yoo, then deputy assistant attorney general, in a memo to the Pentagon almost on the eve of Camp X-ray's opening: "Restricting the President's plenary power over military operations (including the treatment of prisoners) would be constitutionally dubious."

It was developed more fully in Bybee's memo the following August. He asserted that this was the plan of the Republic's founders all along, quoting the first U.S. treasury secretary Alexander Hamilton's arguments when he advocated the states' adoption of the federal Constitution: "The circumstances which may affect the public safety are not reducible within certain limits . . . there can be no limitation of the authority, which is to provide for the defense and protection of the community."

This authority, Bybee said, was exercised by the President: "The structure of the Constitution demonstrates that any power traditionally understood as pertaining to the executive—which includes the conduct of warfare and the defense of the nation . . . is vested in the President . . . national security decisions require the unity in purpose and energy in action that characterize the Presidency rather than Congress." From this, Bybee boldly leapt to the conclusion that any restrictions on interrogations or the use of torture were unconstitutional: "Just as statutes that order the President to conduct warfare in a certain manner or for specific goals would be unconstitutional, so too are laws that seek to prevent the President from gaining the intelligence he believes necessary to prevent attacks upon the United States."

The first report of the Pentagon's working group on interrogation methods made the argument again in March 2003, this time casting it so as to protect American interrogators asked to torture captives: "As this authority is inherent in the President, exercise of it by subordinates would be best if it can be shown to have been derived from the President's authority through Presidential directive or other writing."

In this reading of the Constitution, the separation of powers has given way to a new form of absolutism; something close to a divine right of presidents. We have already met General Boykin, and the religiosity of the Bush White House is a matter of record. Attorney General Ashcroft, Bybee's boss when he wrote his memo, begins his day with a prayer meeting for staff. "We are a nation called to defend freedom—a freedom that is not the grant of any government or document but is our endowment from God," Ashcroft told the National Religious Broadcasters' Convention in February 2002. "Our fight against terrorism is a defense of our freedom in the most profound sense: It is the defense of our right to make moral choices—to seek fellowship with God." Ashcroft was sure that with his assistance, America would succeed in its mission "to use the law to defend itself from barbarians and remain civilized."

The Gitmo system and the arguments used to underpin it suggest that these outward signs of a belief in divine endorsement of President Bush are more than mere trappings, and they put America in malignant company. The horrors of the midtwentieth century were perpetrated by regimes that while atheist in nature, were equally convinced of the justice of their cause against external enemies, and considered themselves immune to independent scrutiny. Nazi Germany smashed the authority of civilian courts in the name of the *fuhrerprinzip,* with the creation of special tribunals for political crimes and automatic authorization for the "third degree" in interrogations of those it deemed its enemies: listed by the S.S. chief Heinrich Himmler, these were "communists, Marxists, Jehovah's Witnesses, saboteurs, terrorists, members of resistance movements and antisocial elements." From the moment Lenin published his *What Is to Be Done* in 1902, with its contemptuous rejection of the concept of "freedom" as a "grand word" under whose banner "the most predatory wars were waged . . . [and] the working people were robbed," the history of the Russian revolution is, in one sense, a story of the rejection of the separation of powers in favor of dictatorship and its Soviet consequence, the *gulag*.

Past American presidents have tried to assume such exceptional powers in wartime, and all have eventually been overruled by the Supreme Court: among the best-known examples is Abraham Lincoln's attempt to suspend the right of habeas corpus during the Civil War. In a 1967 case about rights to protest during the Vietnam War, Chief Justice Warren observed, "The concept of 'national defense' cannot be deemed an end in itself, justifying any exercise . . . of power designed to promote such a goal. Implicit in the term 'national defense' is the notion of defending those values and ideals which set this nation apart."

An earlier ringing statement of principle was made by Justice Jackson, who had been America's prosecutor at Nuremburg, the man who cross-examined Hermann Goering in the excerpt quoted at the beginning of this book. Handing down his opinion in the 1952 case *Youngstown Sheet and Tube Co. v. Sawyer,* Jackson recalled the example of the constitution of the Weimar republic, which gave its president powers "to suspend any or all individual rights if public safety and order were seriously disturbed or endangered. This proved a temptation to every government, whatever its shade of opinion, and in 13 years suspension of rights was invoked on more than 250 occasions. Finally, Hitler persuaded President Von Hindenberg to suspend all such rights, and they were never restored."

Such an usurpation must never be permitted in America, Justice Jackson said, even in time of war. "The claim of inherent and unrestricted presidential powers has long been a persuasive dialectical weapon in political controversy." But "the essence of our free Government is 'leave to live by no man's leave, underneath the law'—to be governed by those impersonal forces which we call law. Our Government is fashioned to fulfill this concept so far as humanly possible. With all its defects, delays and inconveniences, men have discovered no technique for long preserving free government except that the Executive be under the law, and that the law be made by parliamentary deliberations."

Its creators having cast these principles aside, the Gitmo system exists in a topsy-turvy world, where words, as well as constitutions, can reverse their ordinary meanings. Item: "We will adhere to the provisions of the Geneva Convention" means, in Gitmo-speak, "we will breach the Geneva Convention." The claim that "detainees are treated humanely" ought to be translated so: "Detainees are treated inhumanely." The Pentagon's claim that detainees will be tried fairly by military commission was exploded by Lieutenant Commander Swift: "Think of it as a medieval joust, turned into a sketch from Monty Python. They're riding a huge charger, armed with a sword and a lance. I'm trying to block them, standing on the ground, waving a little stick." Yet all of this has been done in the name of freedom and democracy, for the values expressed by Major General Miller's Gitmo motto: "Honor bound to defend freedom."

In the minds of the administration's ideologists, the shrug-

ging-off of the straitjacket of international law is a virtue in and
of itself, evidence of America's exceptionalism, proof of its manifest destiny in the twenty-first century. A version of this mani-
festo is found at the end of *An End to Evil: How to Win the War on
Terror,* the 2003 polemic by former White House speechwriter
David Frum (author of Bush's January 2002 "axis of evil" State of
the Union address) and Richard Perle, assistant defense secretary
under President Reagan, and, as the Gitmo system was being
conceived, chairman of the Pentagon's Defense Policy Advisory
Board.

After citing numerous examples of the perceived failure of
the international system, they write that the United Nations has
"traduced the dream" that created it: "A world at peace; a world
governed by law; a world in which all peoples are free to find
their own destinies: That dream has not yet come true, it will not
come true soon, but if it ever does come true, it will be brought
into being by American armed might and defended by American
armed might, too. Our vocation is to support justice with power.
It is a vocation which has earned us terrible enemies. It is a vocation that has made us, at our best moments, the hope of the
world."

On June 28, 2004, the Supreme Court of the United States began
to fill in the legal black hole in which Guantánamo Bay had existed for the previous thirty months. The lead plaintiff in the
landmark case of *Rasul v. Bush* was none other than Shafiq Rasul
of Tipton, joined by Asif Iqbal, the Australians Mamdouh Habib
and David Hicks, and twelve Kuwaiti charity workers who said
they had first been captured by Afghan bounty hunters. In blunt,
undemonstrative language, Justice Paul Stevens and five of his

colleagues demolished the argument by which the administration had justified the denial of legal and constitutional rights to foreign detainees—the claim that because Gitmo was leased from Cuba, the right an alien in America would have had to demand habeas corpus and other protections did not apply there.

The justices did lack awareness of the historic importance of what they had to say. Citing Magna Carta, they recalled: "Executive imprisonment has been held oppressive and lawless since John, at Runnymede, pledged that no free man should be imprisoned, dispossessed, outlawed or exiled save by a judgement of his peers or the law of the land." The precedent advanced by the government had been a Supreme Court ruling from 1949, which held that six World War II German spies captured and tried by military commission in China did not have a right to American habeas corpus review. But their situation, Steven's opinion stated, was completely different from that of the detainees at Gitmo. It was clear that habeas did apply to Americans there, and the law contained nothing to suggest that its applicability depended on a person's citizenship. "Aliens held at the base, no less than American citizens, are entitled to invoke the federal courts' authority." The consequences were immediate, and from the administration's perspective, explosive. Any detainee had the right to challenge the basis of his imprisonment in an American federal court and to see a civilian lawyer at Gitmo.

Within a week of the judgment being issued, the first five of what, at the time of writing in July 2004, seems certain to be a flood of habeas petitions had already been filed in the district court in Washington, and the Pentagon was being forced to make arrangements for the detainees to see their attorneys. The original *Rasul v. Bush* litigation had been handled by the Center for

Constitutional Rights in New York, the British-born attorney Clive Stafford Smith, supported by the Soros Foundation, and the Washington branch of the big commercial law firm Shearman and Sterling. By the end of the first week of July, another eight such firms were training the big legal guns of their *pro bono* departments on the Bush Administration, on behalf of Gitmo detainees.

Back in February, in an apparent attempt to defuse the pending Supreme Court case, the Pentagon had announced a process of annual "administrative reviews" for prisoners, in which they would be given a chance to explain why they were no longer dangerous, and therefore fit for release. They would not be given legal representation at such "parole" hearings, while the evidence against them would remain largely secret. On July 8, Deputy Defense Secretary Paul Wolfowitz announced that in response to the Supreme Court's ruling, he was setting up special "enemy combatant review" tribunals at Gitmo, in which detainees could challenge the fact that they had been classified as such in the first place. Even as he did so, it was evident that they would be feeble substitutes for a proper court. The tribunals' presumption would be that a detainee's classification as a member of the Taliban or al-Qaeda had always been well founded, and it would be up to him to provide proof to rebut it. In contrast to the Article 5 Geneva Convention tribunals that CENTCOM had envisaged in its own regulations (see chapter one), anyone who applied to go before one of these review tribunals would not get a lawyer, merely the "assistance of a military officer."

With the alternative now available of lodging a petition in federal court, Wolfowitz's kangaroo tribunals did not look like an attractive option. However, the Supreme Court had not specified exactly how detainees should exercise their newfound rights, and the tribunals' creation raised the prospect that argument over the details would soon bog down in further protracted litigation. Most lawyers agreed that Steven's ruling was probably the beginning of the end of the Gitmo system. But in an election year, the administration was keen to avoid the sight of being forced to release hundreds of prisoners who had previously been deemed to be among the most dangerous members of humanity. Its priority now was to drag out the process as long as possible, and in any event, past the presidential ballot of November 2004.

Not only decisions to classify prisoners as enemy combatants, but also the rules of the military commissions would now be open to challenge in federal court, and anyone who was convicted could now appeal to federal judges, not merely to President Bush. "My administrative law professor always used to say, that with law of this kind, you can go slow, or you can go fast," said Charles Swift. "In this case, it seems pretty obvious the government wants to go slow."

There are some signs that celebrations on detainees' behalf may be premature. In another ruling announced the same day as *Rasul,* the Supreme Court considered the case of Yaser Hamdi, an American citizen captured in Afghanistan who had also been detained indefinitely as an enemy combatant—not at Gitmo but at a naval brig in South Carolina. Speaking for the plurality in that case, Justice Sandra Day O'Connor affirmed the President's right to decide whether someone was an unlawful or enemy combatant, and she added observations that may yet come to haunt prisoners at Gitmo: "The Constitution would not be offended by a presumption in favor of the government's evidence . . . once the government puts forward credible evidence that petitioner meets the enemy combatant criteria, the onus could shift to the petitioner to rebut that evidence with more persuasive evidence." As we have seen, it was announced that the Gitmo Wolfowitz tribunals would follow that principle. In the context of Guantánamo, the government's evidence would likely consist of the old, corrupt, "intelligence" material first acquired by the amateurish and inexperienced screening officers in Afghanistan, or coercive interrogations in Cuba. But it is not difficult to see how this might be dressed up as persuasive testimony from classified sources, who would attest to a detainee's support for terrorism. Justice O'Connor added, ominously: "The full protections that accompany challenges to detentions in other settings may prove unworkable and inappropriate in the enemy combatant setting."

As the legal struggles over Guantánamo move into their next phase, far more than the immediate issues at hand are at stake. Lord Steyn, the British law lord, one of the twelve members of the Supreme Court of America's closest ally, described Gitmo in November 2003 as a "monstrous failure of justice," the product of an "unprincipled and exorbitant executive response" to the September 11 attacks. "The purpose of holding the prisoners at Guantánamo Bay was and is to put them beyond the rule of law, beyond the protection of any courts, and at the mercy of the victors," he said. "The question is whether the quality of justice envisaged for the prisoners at Guantánamo Bay complies with minimum international standards for the conduct of fair trials. The answer can be given quite shortly: It is a resounding No. The term kangaroo court springs to mind. It conveys the idea of a preordained, arbitrary rush to judgment by an irregular tribunal which makes a mockery of justice. Trials of the type contemplated by the United States government would be a stain on

United States justice. The only thing that could be worse is simply to leave the prisoners in their black hole indefinitely."

How could an American administration have contemplated and executed such actions, and in so doing, as we have seen, turn its back on the very philosophies that informed the genesis of the nation? The answer has to be that Guantánamo reflects other battles being fought for the soul and direction of American society, deep conflicts that have been aptly described as a "culture war." On the one hand are the secular and constitutional principles of the American republic. On the other is the Christian authoritarianism of Boykin, Ashcroft and Bush, an exceptionalism that for the rest of the world means only the justice of theocratic American might, in some senses a mirror image of the millenarian obscurantism espoused by Osama bin Laden in his mysterious Asian cave.

In *Bush v. Gore,* the Florida election case of 2001, the Supreme Court handed this side victory, in what some have termed a constitutional putsch. In *Rasul v. Bush,* it dealt it a significant defeat.

Yet even if the Gitmo system does start to unravel, its costs have been enormous. "We were supposed to be different," said Lieutenant Commander Swift. "We didn't just talk a good game, we played a good game. We were supposed to be the good guys. But at Gitmo, we aren't. Guantánamo has damaged America tactically and strategically. Even if we did get some intelligence of value, it wasn't worth it. And let's suppose that among those 600 detainees, there are some real bad guys. The likelihood now is that eventually, they'll go free. If we'd handled this differently, this wouldn't have been the case."

There is damage to more than America's reputation. In the

1990s, international lawyers were for a few years seized with optimism: with the tribunals in Rwanda and Sierra Leone and the indictment of Slobodan Milosevic, it was beginning to seem that states could find effective means to collaborate in the name of justice, to use law as a way of making tyrants and terrorists accountable. After Gitmo, that impetus has been scattered to the winds.

The conservative writer Samuel Huntington has famously spoken of a clash of civilizations between the West and Islam, a coming titanic conflict that will drench the world in blood. At Guantánamo, America adopted some of the modes and techniques of those it classed as enemies. In so doing, it has brought Huntington's baleful prophecy nearer to fruition.